contents

introduction

Start with good people, lay out the rules,
communicate with your employees, motivate
them and reward them when they perform.

Lee Iacocca

Management matters. If you have a team of people reporting to
you, then supervising them takes time and needs both consideration and care. It does not matter whether the team is just a
handful of people or an entire organization; the principles are
the same. So too is the measurement that is applied. Your
competence as a manager will be judged not solely on what you
do yourself, though this is doubtless important, but on the
combined performance of you and your team – all of them, in
all their aspects. And there is no doubt that people who are
well motivated perform better than those who are not.

The days of just telling people what to do, if they ever truly
existed, are long gone. Staff are more demanding of their
employers than in the past. They want to know what is going
on, they want to be consulted and they want to be involved.
They want to feel that whatever they do it has some real worth
and they preferably want it to have an element of enjoyment,
certainly of satisfaction. When people are content in these
kinds of ways they will perform well. So, if you motivate your
people well they will perform better than if you do not (and
certainly better than when they feel management is actively

antagonistic in some way). And the incentive for doing so is that a successful team not only gets the job done, whatever that is, but reflects well on whoever manages them also.

Motivation matters. It increases efficiency, effectiveness and productivity, and makes it more likely that whatever results are targeted will be hit. Conversely, its lack increases the time management takes, the endless checking up, argument and hassle that comes the manager's way when people are at a low ebb motivationally – and thus take their eye to some extent off the ball.

Let us be clear. If a group of people is not motivated, the results can specifically include the following:

Increased:

- absenteeism;
- waste of time – breaks, conversation (unrelated to work) and private tasks (from telephoning friends to surfing the Internet);
- gossip and, at worst, active rumour-mongering or disruption of others;
- bucking of the system (eg embellishing claims for expenses);
- challenging of policy;
- bureaucracy.

Reduced:

- care, and thus lower quality of work;
- pace of work;
- willingness to take responsibility;
- level of creative contributions;
- punctuality (eg being late for meetings or finding reasons to go home early);
- attention (eg to management instructions, leading to errors);
- maintenance of the organization culture.

This is a list to which you can doubtless add. The small details are important and any combination of symptoms is possible. The net outcome in terms of results is clear. So too is the way the management job increases and becomes more difficult when motivation is low.

The advantages of good motivation are also clear from the list above (absenteeism is reduced and so on). Again many combinations of advantage may come from it, and much of the success is in the detail. For example, the well-motivated person – one who is prepared to put himself or herself out that much more than others – can make a big difference to results and this can be multiplied by the number in the team.

Being well motivated can also make work more fun, and do so for both motivated and motivator. All in all, motivating people is a key aspect of any manager's job. It is not, as may sometimes be thought, just a 'good thing to do' – it is a tool, like any other, that can directly influence the achievement of results.

The simple formula, shown below, makes the point: performance in all its aspects is inherently tied in with motivation. Any manager ignores the motivation of their people at their peril.

Performance = (Ability + Knowledge) × Motivational Feeling

making it work

So far so good; having a well-motivated team seems desirable. But motivation is not something that can be applied now and then like some sort of magic dust. There is no magic formula. Motivating people successfully takes thought, time and care. What needs to be done is largely a matter of detail. Motivation must be applied through the many and various activities of the management process, as well as using its own particular techniques. It is an active, indeed an ongoing, process.

If this is beginning to hint at complexity then there is some truth to that. The complexity of the process is, however, not because of any major complications – indeed much of what must be done is common sense – it arises only because there is a plethora of different things to consider. This is exaggerated by the fact that most managers already have a good deal to do, and a fair range of different things to do, before they start thinking about the need to motivate people.

If you understand the motivation process, first in terms of the basic human psychology involved, and also by having an ordered and logical 'shopping list' of motivational possibilities that you might deploy, then what must be done becomes straightforward. It may still take time and effort, and it must still be fitted in with other matters. But certain individual actions can become routine – some things can benefit from becoming habit – and in this way some activity can be fitted in without major time commitment. There can then remain time to take a creative view of the process too, for it needs more than routine action. Motivation should not simply satisfy people (sometimes with them hardly being aware that influence is being brought to bear), it should occasionally surprise them.

This book has a simple brief: to set out sufficient details about how and why motivation operates, and to suggest how exactly to build action designed both to negate or reduce negative influences into the management job, and to actively build a suitably positive motivational feeling in people. The ultimate objectives are also clear: productive people willing as well as able to do what is required of them so that targets are hit and, better still, excellence of performance is achieved consistently and reliably.

Motivation is a core skill. Used well it allows managers, and their staff, to achieve more; potentially much more. If you want to be judged a successful manager you must cultivate suitable motivational skills. The rewards are in the results that it helps ensure will follow.

the new realities

The world of work has changed recently (yes, I am sure you have noticed), and it is a truism to say that we live in dynamic times. Nor have all such changes been positive. The press, and business books for that matter, persistently mention: recession, downsizing, redundancy, cutback, lay-off, closure, stress, glass ceiling, and more. They also reflect the reality of changed ways of working: home- and tele-working, short-term contracts and portfolio careers. The good old days of 'jobs for life' have gone, apparently for ever, and all of this can easily prompt regret or even resentment.

But there is all the difference in the world between regretting something and doing something about it. Certainly a very much more planned and active approach to career development than was necessary in the past has become essential for anyone with ambitions to get on in business or organizational life. (My thoughts on this are in *Career Skills: A guide to long term success*, Cassell.) Here the way changes affect the management job are certainly relevant.

Within this context, management probably has a tougher job to do than at any time in the past. The fast pace of technology provides one major ongoing example with the job of coming to terms with, and getting to grips with, new equipment and the processes it involves all the time. The information technology revolution is just a part of that. Though if you are still struggling togettoGRIPS wih* (sic) doing all your own typing on a machine which seemingly has a mind of its own, do not expect sympathy (least of all from me – I have some 40,000 words to go on this!). The benefits may be considerable, but there are real drawbacks and learning curves along the way.

Management therefore has more to cope with than in the past; what it has to cope with is, in many cases, more complex; and at the same time other pressures seem to combine to make life more difficult. Simply too much to do in too little time seems to be a major pressure for many, and this can be compounded by other factors such as downsizing or restricted budgets. The pressure of this sort of thing gives rise to stress, indeed to a whole stress-related industry (at least your stress may be making others happy – think of those [not me] who conduct stress management courses) and so the difficulties mount up.

Managers under pressure, particularly what they see as unreasonable pressure, can respond by taking it out on those nearest them, and in the office this is their staff. Yet they may be under pressure too and the whole difficulty increases as relationships between the two parties decline. Though many, most even, thrive from being under *some* pressure, clearly too much pressure is ultimately likely to affect peoples' performance adversely. This is not the place to suggest remedies for this overall situation.

motivation in context

What is important is the relationship between this sort of reality, and the attitude taken to it and the process of motivation. It is easy to underrate the need to spend time motivating people, and even easier to do so when you are under pressure and could perhaps do with a bit of motivation yourself. Allowing this to happen must be avoided. If times are tough, the pressure is on and still results must be achieved, that is surely precisely the time when you want your staff to be performing well, when you want them to be largely self-sufficient, and when – logically – they must be well-motivated.

The time you spend on the process may be all sorts of things – useful, desirable, 'a good thing' – but it is also cost- and time-effective. It works. Motivating people has a direct link with results. So, ultimately, the reason for doing it – and doing it well – is to help you achieve the results you want. Given the support of your staff it can engender, it may even make your own life a little less stressful.

Now, with an emphasis on office-based staff (though the principles are similar whoever is being managed) we turn to the details any manager needs to bear in mind to be able to actively motivate successfully.

Patrick Forsyth
Touchstone Training & Consultancy
28 Saltcote Maltings
Heybridge
Maldon
Essex CM9 4QP

the motivation process

Motivation is important and makes a difference to results, but just saying or believing this is so does not guarantee that it will be done; much less that it will be done well. If you manage people, think for a moment of your own manager or of those others to whom you have reported in the past. You probably have strong views of them, perhaps they helped you – or hindered you. Their attitude may have been constructive, innovative or they may have driven you mad with what you regarded as an attitude of unnecessary bureaucracy. One lasting impression is surely how your job worked for you as you related with them and how they made you feel about it. The people who work for you will have similar feelings. Motivation is not, however, for all its importance, the only thing a manager must do.

the management task

Managers must manage. But what does that mean? It can be defined as the whole process of *obtaining results through other people*. Managers are judged on the results of their team, not just on the work they do personally. Classically, there are six key management tasks and it is worth thinking about motivation in context of this full description. The key tasks can be defined as:

- planning;
- recruitment and selection;
- organizing;
- training and development;
- motivation;
- control.

These are the main tasks. They must be achieved, of course, through a profusion of activities: communication, problem-solving, decision making, consultation – through to sitting in meetings. And everything, but everything, involves people. Even solo tasks, writing a report for instance, are ultimately concerned with people (unless nobody reads it!).

On the one hand motivation is a particular task, as are the other things that must be done, and one that needs individual care and attention. Here lies one of the problems. Other matters may seem to have greater importance, or rather – for the most part – greater urgency. For instance, imagine that the monthly sales figures are down and you must instigate a crash programme of promotion to rectify matters in a situation where competitors are stepping up their efforts and results are expected by the end of a financial period. Given any such circumstances, then it may be a little difficult to remember to spend some time boosting the feelings of the people who work with you.

On the other hand, motivational feeling can, in part at least, be influenced through all the other activities. What is more, time spent building in some action to motivate people might well help achieve the result. Because motivation goes so tightly hand in hand with other management activities, and because how people perform is so closely linked to how they feel about the work they do, the job of motivating people can become an inherent element of the total management job. To set the scene, an example from each of the main management task areas will help exemplify the point:

■ *Planning:* plan the work and work the plan, as the old saying has it; planning – whether it involves an overall business plan or simply (simply?) a project plan – is ubiquitous in business. Many regard it as a chore; certainly an annual planning exercise can represent a major undertaking, one that is often felt to be primarily for the benefit of senior management. Yet a good plan should make all that follows operationally easier and more certain to achieve (if not why have a plan at all?). And a plan that plays a part in communication, that has a role in spelling out to those down the line how things will work and why, is certainly motivational. So the various effects on others is something that must be accommodated during any planning process.

■ *Recruitment and selection:* few things are more important than assembling an effective team. Although many managers like to claim an infallible ability to judge people, it is in fact no easy task and must be done thoroughly, systematically and with a real element of objectivity. It also constitutes the first opportunity to communicate with those who work with the organization; an effective interview and selection process is remembered and sets the scene for successful candidates in terms of how they feel during their early time working for the organization. If they think well of it, it plays a part in creating their initial motivational feelings. It may influence the feelings of others too, who respect a manager who creates a powerful team, and resent a slapdash approach that adds people to the team who do not pull their weight.

■ *Organizing:* good organization may have to reflect many things: the work to be done, the standards to be set and more. But what is being organized is how people work, and work together, and if organization is also seen to take into account how it affects people personally then it is more likely that they will feel well motivated at least in one respect about their jobs.

■ *Training and development:* this is a prime management responsibility, especially given the current rate of change in the business world and the need to update or add skills in order to maintain a full capability to do a job. Surveys that ask people what they want of an 'ideal' manager will often list 'someone from whom I learn' at or near the top of the list of criteria. There are surely plenty of opportunities in this area not just to instigate necessary development, but to create positive motivation.

■ *Motivation:* some things must be done, and must be seen to be done, in a way that concentrates on the task of motivating. Staff expect attention to be given to this and just working for someone who manifestly cares about the people who work for them, and is at pains to take their situation into account, is itself motivational.

■ *Control:* managers must manage, and that necessarily entails activities to check results (and to take correcting action if things are not going to plan). Even here there are motivational opportunities – if the amount of checking (and therefore the lack of trust) is too much then demotivation results. But a manager who never checks, and is seen as uninterested or uncaring, can also be regarded as less than attractive as a boss.

Under all of the above headings, and through all the many activities that they constitute, motivation will be influenced. It is not a question of *will* management action affect peoples' motivational status – it will – but only of *how* it will be affected. For example, at one course I ran in a large City law firm, I was with a group of recent graduate recruits. This is a specialist area and the job of selecting exactly who is invited to join the firm is vital, yet cannot be easy. I asked if they felt that the recruitment process had been well executed. One member of the group responded instantly, saying he felt it had been less than professional. 'I don't think', he said, 'they really have any idea whether I'm a successful recruitment for them or not.' He might have dismissed such feeling and been simply pleased that he had been successful in joining the firm. But, looking back, the process left him with negative feelings about his new employers, yet it surely could – and perhaps should – have acted to motivate.

Almost every activity a manager engages in will have motivational consequences. The job is to make sure they are good ones. The first step to doing so is to understand something of the psychology involved. Just what is it that motivates people? In fact, as so often is the case, there are two sides to this particular coin. The questions to ask are: What makes people feel good and positive about their employer, particularly their manager, and above all their job and all it entails? And what creates negative feelings? Motivation is essentially the job of creating a balance, one that minimizes those things that might create negative feelings and maximizes those that create positive ones; and doing so in a way that ensures that the positive ones predominate.

What completes the picture is being able not only to create positive motivation, but to link it closely to the jobs to be done, and make the process manageable in terms of both time and money. After all it might be motivational to take the whole team out to a grand lunch every day, but the costs would be prohibitive and the time it took would hardly help ensure productivity.

One caveat is crucial here. Motivation demands honesty and sincerity. It is very difficult to motivate if, in truth, you do not really care about people. Not just caring because they are your people, and your business role and success may be dependent on them – but really caring about them, for themselves. Thus if you even appear insincere it will negate or seriously dilute any good you might do motivationally.

Conversely, if you do really care, motivation is easy. Well, it may still be difficult to find time for everything and to leave no stone unturned and do a thorough job, but it will be easy in the sense that it demands no more than that you follow your instincts: set people clear objectives and goals. Make them want to strive for them and communicate with them all the way through, especially telling them when they succeed. The quotation which heads the Introduction from Lee Iacocco (at the time CEO of Chrysler) is very apposite; it is almost QED – in principle perhaps, but success is in the details. In the next chapter we investigate a little theory, with an eye firmly on how an understanding of this helps in selecting and taking action to influence people positively.

how people feel about work

In theory there is no difference between theory and practice. In practice there is.

Yogi Berra

There used to be a school of thought that how people felt about work was not an issue. The work was what mattered and managers took the view that getting performance from staff was a straightforward process. You told them what to do, and they did it. Period. And if that was, for some reason, insufficient then it was backed by the power of management; in effect by coercion.

Management by fear still exists. It has its counterpart in every field. For example, in one of the early Bond films, 007 is being pursued by a group of villains whose leaders encourage their pursuit with the thought: 'The man that gets him stays alive.' In the organizational world things may not be that ruthless, though in any economy with less than full employment the ultimate threat is being out of a job. Everyday threats may be subtle or specific, just an exaggerated form of arm-twisting or out-and-out bullying (and it might be as simple as the threat of being given unpalatable tasks or left out of something interesting). Even if such tactics work (at least short term) – they are resented.

The manager's job is not simply to get things done: it is to get things done *willingly*. Make no mistake. The resentment factor is considerable. People fight against anything they consider to be an unreasonable demand. So much so that the fighting may tie up a fair amount of time and effort, with performance ending up as only the minimum that people 'think they can get away with'.

Only if people *want* to do things and are encouraged to do things well can they be relied on to actually do them really well. Motivation provides reasons for people to want to deliver good performance.

If this sounds no more than common sense, then that is because it is. For example, are you more likely to read the rest of this book if I tell you that if you do not I will come round to your house and break all your windows, or if I persuade you that you will find doing so really useful and offer you some sort of tangible reward? (I do intend you will find it useful, incidentally, but sadly there is no free holiday on offer.) Motivation works because it reflects something about human nature, and understanding the various theories that relate to it is a useful prerequisite to deploying motivational techniques. This is an area where much is based on research.

theory X and theory Y

This intriguing concept stems from the first of the motivational theories that is worthy of some note and was documented by Douglas McGregor. He defined the human behaviour relevant to organizational life in two contrasting ways as follows:

■ *Theory X:* makes the assumption that people are lazy, uninterested in work or responsibility and thus must be pushed and cajoled in order to get anything done in a disciplined way, with reward assisting the process to some degree.

■ *Theory Y*: takes the opposite view. It assumes people want to work. They enjoy achievement, gain satisfaction from responsibility and are naturally inclined to seek ways of making work a positive experience.

There is truth in both pictures. What McGregor was doing was describing the extreme positions which people can take. Of course, there are jobs that are inherently boring and mundane, and others that are obviously more interesting, and it is no surprise that it is easier to motivate those doing the latter. Though having said that, it is really a matter of perspective. There is an old and apocryphal story of a despondent group of convicts breaking rocks being asked about their feelings concerning the backbreaking work. All expressed negative feelings, except one – who said simply 'It makes it bearable if I keep the end result in mind – I'm helping to build a cathedral.' Research shows that most people will respond to anything that makes their work life more interesting. An experiment in a production-line situation rearranged people into teams working against the clock in competition with each other. The team who completed their allotted task first announced this to all by ringing a bell; and an old ship-style bell was put at the end of the line for this purpose. There was nothing else – no bonuses or rewards of any sort – but productivity increased markedly. It presumably provided some interest – at least for the moment – within a mundane environment, and people do, for the most part respond in that way.

Whether you favour Theory X or Theory Y – and Theory Y is surely more attractive – it is suggested that motivation creates a process that draws the best from any situation. Some motivation can help move people from a Theory X situation to a Theory Y one; thereafter it is easier to build on positive Theory Y principles to achieve still better motivational feeling and still better performance. It certainly creates thoughts worth bearing in mind, among others.

Maslow's hierarchy of needs

People's needs are considered by another theory that helps describe the basic situation in which all motivational effort must be directed: that of Abraham Maslow. He wrote that people's needs are satisfied progressively. In other words, only when basic needs are met do their aspirations rise and are other goals set.

The first, most basic, such needs are psychological: having enough to eat and drink, warmth, shelter and rest. In a working environment people need to earn sufficient to buy the answers to these. Next come the needs of safety and protection: ranging from job security (one that is less easily met than once was the case) to good health (with the provision of healthcare schemes by employers now very common).

Beyond that Maslow described social needs: all those associated with working in groups with other people. The work environment is a social environment, indeed for some people it may represent the majority of the people contact in their lives. Linked to these is a further level of needs, such as recognition within the organization and among all those people comprising the work environment. Also the ability to feel self-confidence and self-fulfilment, and to look positively to a better future, one in which we are closer to realizing our perceived potential and are happier because of it.

However you define and describe this theory, it is the hierarchical nature of it that is important. What it says, again wholly sensibly, is that people's motivations can only be satisfied if this hierarchy is respected. For instance, it suggests that motivational input is doomed to be ineffective if it is directed at one level when a lower one is unsatisfied. It is thus of little use to tell people how satisfying a job is if they are consumed with the thought that the low rate of pay makes them unable to afford basic essentials.

Again this does not describe the whole process in a way that you can use as is to create the right motivation in your office, but it helps show one element of what is involved. Table 2.1 illustrates a little more about this theory and shows how it provides useful background to active motivation.

Table 2.1   *The hierarchy of motivational needs*

- Self-actualization needs (how you regard yourself and how you are regarded);
- Ego needs (how other people acknowledge you and what you do);
- Social needs (friends and personal contacts of all sorts);
- Safety needs (eg job security);
- Physiological needs (the basics of food, warmth, etc).

People's needs move up the column, with concentration being on the more basic things first, then finally on all those things that reflect our satisfaction with fulfilling our potential (self-actualization needs). At the very least we must recognize how these basic instincts are affected by the work environment. For example, with job security less now than was the case in the past, other forms of security become more important. Similarly, people's need to work and interact with others affects how they see teams, groups and the many organizational aspects of modern enterprises. New developments and new ways of doing things may well change people's attitudes in a way that reflects back to this hierarchy of needs. One example will perhaps help make the point. Computer systems of the sort used by those working in call centres change the nature of the human contact they have at work; that with customers becomes much more proscribed and that with colleagues is minimized in the interests of productivity. This does not make motivation impossible, but it does change somewhat the motivational job to be done.

Hertzberg's motivator/hygiene factors

More important in a day-to-day sense, and certainly more of an immediate spur to action that creates positive motivation is this third theory. Frederick Hertzberg described two categories of factor: first, the *hygiene factors* – those that switch people off if they cause negative feelings. And secondly, the *motivators*, factors that can make people feel good. Consider these in turn.

the dissatisfiers (or hygiene factors)

These he listed as follows:

- company policy and administrative processes;
- supervision;
- working conditions;
- salary;
- relationship with peers;
- personal life (and the impact of work on it);
- status;
- security.

All are external factors that affect the individual (because of this they are sometimes referred to as *environmental* factors). When things are without problem in these areas, all is well motivationally. If there are problems they all contain considerable potential for diluting the prevailing motivational feeling.

Note: it should be noted here, in case perhaps it surprises you, that salary comes in this list. It is a potential dissatisfier. Would you fail to raise your hand in answer to the question: Would you like to earn more money? Most people would certainly say 'yes'. At a particular moment an existing salary may be acceptable (or unacceptable), but it is unlikely to turn you on and be a noticeable part of your motivation. So too for those who work for you – more of this later.

It is, for instance, things in these areas that give rise to gripes and dissatisfaction. Such are often not momentary upsets, they can rumble on. If the firm's parking scheme fails to work and you always find someone else in your place, perhaps someone more senior who it is difficult to dislodge, it rankles and the feeling is always with you. Or if a colleague's persistent slowness holds up your work and ability to hit deadlines, or if the volume of what you regard as unnecessary paperwork increases *again* ... but you can no doubt identify examples all too easily.

There are, as we will see later, many things springing from these areas for managers to work from, and getting them right can assist the process of making a positive contribution to boosting the motivational climate. The restriction here is that these things are not those that can add powerfully to positive motivational feeling. Get things right here and demotivation is avoided. To add more – specifically something positive – you have to turn to Hertzberg's second list.

the satisfiers (or motivators)

These define the key factors that create positive motivation. They are, in order of such power:

- achievement;
- recognition;
- the work itself;
- responsibility;
- advancement;
- growth.

It is all these factors, whether positive or negative and stemming from the intrinsic qualities of human nature, that offer the best opportunities of being used by management to play their part in ensuring that people want to perform and perform well.

expectancy theory

There is one further formal basis for motivation that is worth keeping in mind, and that is what Victor Vroom christened 'expectancy theory'. This states some principles linked to the achievement of goals. First, there is, or can be, a virtuous circle involved here, as – with clear goals in mind – activities lead to their achievement and the liking for achieving those results both spurs people towards them and continues the process as new goals are set.

This is illustrated simply in Figure 2.1.

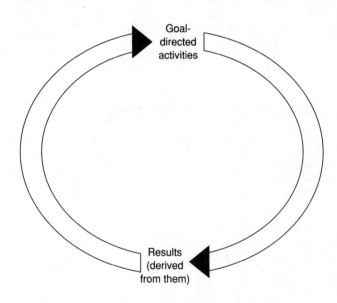

Figure 2.1 *Activities directed towards goals*

This is no more than common sense perhaps, but what expectancy theory says is that the positive effect is multiplied in proportion to the degree to which goals are seen as attainable. Tell me to run a mile in four minutes and the achievement of the task is so mind-bendingly unlikely that I will put little or no effort into it. Tell me to amble down to the pub to meet you in half an hour and, even if that means striding out a bit, it is both possible, desirable and likely to be done. These are, of course, extremes. In fact, what people seem to have in mind is a smooth scale (see Figure 2.2) and what the manager needs to be concerned about is the difference between different points on the scale.

The theory does not preclude managers having high expectations, or setting high targets, but it does mean watching – and

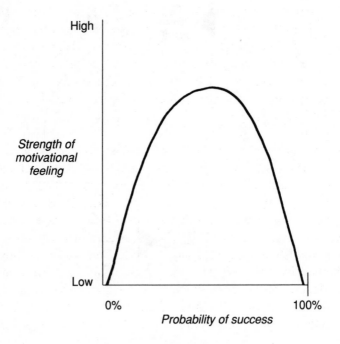

Figure 2.2   *Impact of probability of success on motivation*

influencing – the view people take of them. Persuade people that they can excel and you may well find they can and will. This is not just theory, but something that can be used and worked with. You should bear in mind that:

■ Individuals vary in their own beliefs and feelings; each may need different stimulus in order to succeed and this is one of the factors that make blanket motivation less effective.

■ Often it is internal satisfactions that turn people on, and many are not dramatically affected by external symbols or even money (witness the many jobs that offer poor returns but are viewed as being vocations because they allow a more personal level of satisfaction).

■ Timing is important. A considerable task may seem daunting at the beginning, the belief in success is not there and people balk at it. Motivation at this stage can get people off to a good start, then early success and increasing feelings that success may well be possible after all keep their enthusiasm up as the task is completed.

Thus, to summarize: given a basic belief that effort affects action, that actions dictate results, and that those results are actually desirable in some way (if only as a target to hit), then motivation acts as a catalyst to ensure greater effort is made. Even something like meeting a tight deadline responds to this kind of thinking. It may initially seem impossible. If what is to be achieved is made to seem worth while, and we are enthused – whether by the rewards or the challenge (or both) and persuaded that it is possible – then we get down to it and may surprise ourselves by doing it with less problem than we anticipated. If you understand that this kind of thinking is ubiquitous within your team, you can use that knowledge to help produce greater effort. It occurs to me that perhaps that is why the publisher's deadline for delivering the manuscript for this book was so tight. They would not be so devious – would they? But I digress.

practical implications

It may seem from what has been said already that motivation is a complex business. To some extent this is so. Certainly it is a business affected by many, and disparate, factors. The list of factors affecting motivation, for good or ill, may be long, and that is where any complexity lies, but the process of linking to them in terms of action is often straightforward.

The very nature of people, and how their motivation can be influenced, suggests five important principles for the manager dedicated to actively motivating people. These are:

1. *There is no magic formula* – no one thing, least of all money, provides an easy option to creating positive motivation at a stroke, and anything that suggests itself as such a panacea should be viewed with suspicion.

2. *Success is in the details* – good motivation comes from minimizing the factors that tend to create dissatisfaction, and maximizing the effect of those factors that can create positive motivation. *All of them* in both cases must be considered; it is a process of leaving no stone unturned, with all those found able to contribute to the overall picture being useful to utilize. At the end of the day, what is described as the motivational climate of an organization, department or office is the sum of all the pluses and minuses in terms of how individual factors weigh in the balance.

3. *Continuity* – the analogy of climate is a good one. As a small-scale example of this, consider a greenhouse.

Many factors contribute to the temperature inside. Heating, windows, window blinds, whether a door or window is open, if heating is switched on and so on, all do so. But some such things – whatever they are – are in place and contributing to the prevailing temperature *all the time*. So too with motivation. Managers must accept that creating and maintaining a good motivational climate takes some time and is a continuous task. Anything, perhaps everything, they do can have motivational side-effects. For example, a change of policy may involve a new system and its use may have desirable effects (saving money say), but if the process of complying with the system is seen as bureaucratic and time-consuming the motivational effect may be negative despite results being changed for the better. Overall the trick of successful motivation is to spend the minimum time in such a way as to secure the maximum positive effect.

4. *Timescale* – another thing that must be recognized is the differing timescales involved here. On the one hand signs of low motivation can be a good early warning of performance in peril. If you keep your ear to the ground you may be able to prevent negative shifts in performance or productivity by letting signs of demotivation alert you to the coming problem. The level of motivation falls first, performance follows. Similarly, watch the signs after you have taken action aimed at affecting motivation positively. Performance may take a moment to start to change for the better, but you may well be able to identify that this is likely through the signs of motivation improving. Overreacting because things do not change instantly may do more harm than good. If motivation is improving, performance improvement is usually not far behind. Figure 2.3 shows, in graphic form, what happens in this regard.

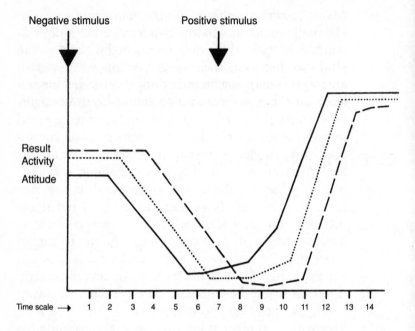

Figure 2.3 *Time relationship of impacts on motivational balance*

5. *Bear others in mind* – there is a major danger in taking a censorious view of any motivational factor – positive or negative. Most managers find that some at least of the things that worry their staff, or switch them on for that matter, are not things that would affect themselves. No matter. It is the other people who matter. If you regularly find things that you are inclined to dismiss as not of any significance, be careful. What matters to you is not the same as what matters to others. If you discover something that can act to assist you build motivation, however weird or trivial it may seem, use it. Dismissing it out of hand, just because it is not something that is important to you, will simply

remove one factor that might help influence the motivational climate and make achieving what you want just a little more difficult. At worst, it will also result in your being seen as uncaring. Similarly, what is important to you may not be important to others. This is a key factor that any manager forgets at his or her peril.

aiming for excellence

Finally in this chapter, remember that even the best performance can often be improved. Motivation is not simply about ensuring that what should happen does happen. It is about striving for – and achieving – excellence. All sorts of things contribute, from the original calibre of the staff you recruit to the training you give them, but motivation may be the final spur that creates exceptional performance where there would otherwise be only satisfactory performance.

It is an effect worth seeking; and it is one multiplied by the number of staff involved. How much more can be achieved by ten, twenty or more people all trying just that bit harder, than can be by one manager, however well intentioned, doing a bit more? Indeed, sometimes managers spend time working furiously to add their effort to the achievement of results, when some of that time applied to helping increase the productivity of a whole group would affect results much more. This is a most acute danger when things are running behind and there is pressure to catch up. Motivation makes a real difference.

the negative side of the balance

How does all this theory relate to the way you manage? You can affect things from both ends as it were. In this chapter we review how to keep the negative issues under control, leaving accentuating the positive until the next chapter, but bearing in mind that both sides must be worked on to create the end result you want.

Immediately we see how motivation works through the details. There is a list of factors (itemized in the last chapter) all of which must be considered. Each, in turn, gives rise to a variety – a plethora – of areas to consider. All of these must be dealt with on the one hand to minimize any negative effect, and on the other to seek what positive impact is possible here. These factors were listed in order of significance, and will be commented on in that way.

company policy and administration

No one likes unnecessary administration or bureaucracy. And

this is especially true when it affects them personally in a restrictive way or gives rise to unfairness. Usually as a manager you have two areas to worry about here. First, the circumstances of *your own department*. Here the task is to consider the motivational implications of every policy and administrative procedure you have in place or instigate. Every form that speeds efficiency may have downsides for those completing it. Every policy, however practical, may do harm as well as good.

For example, a control system may be necessary, but the paperwork involved may be a real chore. If people do not understand the necessity and the advantages that may flow from it (perhaps because no one has explained) they will hate completing it – and may do so in a way that is incomplete or late. The impact will be worse if they feel no effort has been made to keep the system simple.

Every element of every system should be thought through to ensure any demotivation is minimized. And systems must be monitored regularly to make sure they do not get out of date. Time passing and circumstances changing may make any system less effective, so review is necessary apart from the consideration of motivational impact.

Note: one useful tip: always have a review date on any form you instigate or use. For example, if you create a new form, put a date on it (say six months or whatever ahead) and put it in a 'bring forward' file. It then jumps out asking as it were whether it is working well or needs amending (or scrapping). In this way everything gets reviewed regularly and motivation should not suffer from something out-of-date and causing aggravation being unseen and not mentioned.

The second circumstance to concern yourself with is the organization as a whole. Here the task is less to ensure that systems are right for your people – they may be instigated elsewhere – than it is one of communication.

It may be necessary to explain – and endorse – central policies and systems (even those you do not like). It may also be necessary to make suggestions, in a way that acts in both the short and long term, to condition the effect on your people. Staff will always regard you as a weak, perhaps uncaring, manager if you apparently do nothing about matters that clearly inconvenience people or (which can happen) actually make it more difficult for them to do their jobs. Thus maintaining motivation includes fighting your corner for your section, even if this means difficult communications with more senior people. Again this is a matter of continuous review and action.

positive use of policy and administration

The examples that follow both show the extent of this area and give ideas of the action possible:

- ■ forms;
- ■ procedures;
- ■ systems;
- ■ standing instructions;
- ■ rules (eg about personal telephone calls, clocking in, dress codes or uniforms, protective clothing, cleaning of clothes, purchase of company products at a discount, etc).

This is an area where every individual manager in every separate organization can doubtless compile a long list. Those quoted above merely aim to start that process.

supervision

If you are a manager, then supervision means you. How you work, and particularly how you interact with others, especially those who report directly to you, will influence the motivational climate. And it can do so for good or ill. No manager, however personable they believe they are, can assume that people will simply love working for them because it is just wonderful to do so.

This area needs conscious thought and action too. Ideally management style should sit comfortably with the kind of people being managed. It is mentioned here to put it in its appropriate place on the overall balance; it is reviewed in more detail as we proceed.

interpersonal relationships

There are groups of people within some organizations whose job is to get on with their own work and who have little interaction with others. More often teamwork – and the attendant communication, consultation and so on that goes with it – is important, and even if it is not, people will create social interactions because they like them.

A manager must work to try to create a team who, by and large, enjoy working together and make sure that none of the overlaps between people cause problems or rankle in any way. Because of the nature of people this too is a full-time job. No group is wholly untroubled by friction, indeed some friction may well be constructive, but it needs to be kept in proportion.

How interpersonal relationships work starts with the way a team is put together – with recruitment and selection – and goes on throughout every aspect of their working together. It would be wrong to say that every group needs to be made up of similar individuals (again variety can be constructive and creative), but obvious clashes should be avoided. Such could be one young member of one sex in a group which is otherwise older and of the other sex. Or it might be one commuter always rushing for their train in the evening when the group thrives on a little social activity that overlaps the end of the day and spans office and pub. Examples such as these are selected to illustrate the range of factors potentially involved.

positive use of interpersonal relationships

Some examples of factors can be used to create or stimulate communications between groups and around an organization are:

- ■ notice boards and company newsletters or magazines;
- ■ canteens or group refreshment centres;
- ■ resource centres;
- ■ library and information offices;
- ■ social clubs, health clubs or similar facilities;
- ■ Christmas, special occasion or anniversary celebrations;
- ■ counselling services (for a range of things from overeating to outplacement);
- ■ quality circles (or other review or consultation groups).

An individual manager may be able to offer specific stimulus to the process, for example mixing technical and sales staff for product briefing meetings, or arranging a tour of certain departments for those who must liaise with them but do not normally visit them.

working conditions

Productivity and efficiency are directly affected by how people work, and that in turn is affected by their work situation. Space, equipment and everything from air conditioning to whether chairs are comfortable all have an effect.

Here again, while no one expects every job to come with its own plush office, hot and cold running secretaries and unlimited expenses, people are demotivated if conditions are allowed uncaringly to make doing a good job more difficult. Expectations are affected by prevailing practice. For instance, you will readily think of equipment that has moved from being an exception to being 'essential', and is now resented if it is not there: for example mobile telephones, laptop computers, etc.

Working conditions can be changed radically. For instance, some organizations claim dramatic increases in both productivity and motivation from what is called 'hot-desking' (no individual workstations, and a much more organized and integrated open-plan environment); this shows just how broad an area this heading encompasses.

Everything that goes with the job should be included here, from whether you use machines or have a travelling 'tea lady' to how well various systems work. One item that is worth individual mention is the company car. Those who do not have one may regard those who do with envy. Surely any reasonable car is better than none? Not so. Company cars are a major source of dissatisfaction. Everyone who has one wants a better one, or wants it changed more often or to be allowed more choice in the make and model. Any seeming unfairnesses are quickly spotted – *Why does he have that car? He only does a few thousand miles a year and here am I pounding up and down the motorway in a clapped-out...*

This is a matter of status as well as practicality, a good example of how certain factors have motivational implications in a number of different ways. So the moral must be to set, and explain, policy very clearly in this area, watch it like a hawk and do not expect motivational miracles because a car is a given. Cars in unexpected areas, however, may have a strong positive effect. I know managers who give their secretaries a small car, and gain considerable loyalty, retention and long-term cost saving as a result. Be vigilant too about the tax implications of giving a company car; the rules can change and may negate any initial advantage.

personal life

None of the best or most interesting jobs are, in my experience, nine to five (if you know of one, let me know!). But if a job makes unreasonable or unfair inroads into people's private lives this will be resented. Prevailing practice is important here. If certain jobs typically make high demands this may be regarded as normal, and this may mean people put up with it; but it does not mean they like it.

Organizations have to expect people to work hard in a competitive world, but there are limits. Eventually, if things are overdone, productivity will tail down. There is, after all, a considerable difference between activity and achievement. Some people spend extra hours in the office, but not all of these are the most productive. It can become a sort of macho leapfrog with everyone trying to outdo others by being seen at their desks for longer and longer periods of time, but without any productivity gain occurring. The balance needs watching.

So too does the match between people and jobs. Is someone married, single, do they have a young family? All such factors change the way in which the overlap between job and working life is regarded and need a eye keeping on them; travel is just one example of something that might be regarded very differently by different people.

Managers should remember that staff are people with lives outside their work (really!). They like it if you acknowledge this, remembering and commenting on birthdays, asking how the children did in exams and buying a bottle of 'bubbly' when someone does something special – which might range from getting engaged to passing their driving test.

security

Job security may or may not be motivational (some people want more risk if it produces greater rewards). But this is not the sense in which the word is used here. People like security in a variety of ways, and if it is not manifested in those ways they will be demotivated. This gives the manager another area to keep an eye on and to juggle with in order to achieve the desired effect. For example, a degree of security comes from:

- an organization with a clear mission and good communications;
- clear job descriptions and terms of reference;
- knowing what is expected of us and how it is measured;
- working in an (effective) team;
- working for the right kind of manager;
- decisive leadership;
- no unnecessary secrecy.

Let me add a further comment about job descriptions. These are important, and not just because Personnel says everyone must have one. They set the scene for clear job purpose and communication; it is useful if everyone within a department sees everyone else's – and yours. They should collectively spell out how people must work together, where overlaps occur and are *working documents* that may often be useful day to day as much as they are part of the formal systems of the whole organization. If necessary, two versions can be created, one for Personnel purposes (which might have information that is regarded as confidential on it), and another designed as a working tool.

You can doubtless add to the list here. Again the canvass here is considerable, and security is inherently fragile. For example, one decision held up behind closed doors with no explanation can dilute security and escalate rumours very quickly. Yet there may be nothing sinister at work, and it might have taken only a moment to ensure the incident was not seen in this way and thereby avoid the effect.

status

Like security, this can be a largely hidden aspect of people's motivation, but that does not mean it is unimportant; rather the reverse. People want to be thought of as important, doing something worthwhile. If necessary people will create their own status (remember the rock breaker building a cathedral). It happens too on production lines, where people – if they are not switched off completely – will often tell others just how vital their particular bit of the operation is.

So you need to worry about where people sit, how respect for age, seniority, achievement or long service is shown, what they are called and so on. A manager must create respect for his or her people within an organization. This involves communication. A customer being told by a switchboard that a sales representative is not in (something the caller probably expected) because – *they're only a salesman* – is neither well briefed nor helping raise the status of a colleague in the eyes of a customer. Someone, with insufficient authority, who regularly must respond to things by saying 'I must ask my manager' may very well feel of low status, however important their role may be operationally.

Problems may be deeply buried in this area. I once came across someone deeply demotivated because their spouse (who worked in a different field and company) had been promoted and now had 'Manager' on their business card, while they did not. It took a while for their manager to get to the bottom of it.

salary

Yes, this is on the negative side of the balance. Are you that rare person who is totally happy with their current salary? More likely you would like it to be higher. *Existing* salary is rarely motivational. And if it is unfair (internally), out of line with similar jobs elsewhere or otherwise open to real criticism, then it can be a major demotivational factor. In one company I know, salaries are regarded as completely open: anyone can go into the Accountant's office and ask what anyone else earns – and be told. The main effect of this is to act as a control on how salaries are being set – there is no unfairness there, or gripes. I do not suggest this is right for every organization; but it bears a thought.

Another example which says something about how salaries work is the following: freezing salaries for a year can give rise to two years of festering resentment (and thus needs a very good reason). As manager you may be paid to worry about the long term – the financial year. But if some of your staff, especially those who are younger, think Friday week is a long way off, then such long spans of time will be regarded very differently by them than they are by you.

So, motivation cannot be boosted, certainly long term, simply by throwing money at it. Of course, salary (in fact, total remuneration) is important. But it must be considered, just like every other factor, as part of a complex mix – contributing to the ultimate balance along with the other factors.

But you do not need to write off salary completely. A salary *increase*, especially one awarded for merit, is certainly motivational (and we return to that in the next chapter).

the positive side of the balance

While there are plenty of potential negative areas to be avoided, and allowing even seemingly simple factors to dilute motivational feeling is a real danger, there is no lack of positive factors that can be used to actively boost good feelings. As in the last chapter we will use the list of headings originated by Hertzberg, commenting on each in turn to see how they act and how they can be used in a practical sense.

achievement

Everyone gets a kick from achieving something. I was pleased to finish writing the last chapter and press 'Save' (and look forward to finishing this one). There may be very many such small, private satisfactions during your own day's work. There will also be much greater factors (I will be even more pleased when the first printed copy of this book lands on my desk with an – albeit modest! – cheque), and such factors go right through to the satisfaction of a whole financial year being well concluded.

Achievement is relative. Small things can assume a disproportionate importance, and that is fine – to an extent too
people create their own satisfaction, though it is important that
you provide people with sufficient benchmarks to have something to measure achievement against. Targets, formal and
informal, are part of this. They can be linked to almost
anything, and provide a wide range of possibilities, for example
such formal things as:

- ■ the amount a sales person sells (something that can be
  measured in a number of ways – by revenue, by
  numbers of product sold, per week, per month – and
  in a variety of combinations of detail, eg sales of one
  product in the range/in a particular month/to major
  customers/in a specific region);
- ■ the quality and timing of work done;
- ■ how well staff are trained or retained (which could
  produce both long- and short-term measurement);
- ■ cost saving (in terms of actual monetary figures,
  percentages, with links to specific areas or time
  periods);
- ■ speed and efficiency (everything from how promptly
  telephones are answered to how reporting procedures
  are implemented);
- ■ measures of productivity;
- ■ customer satisfaction (which can be measured in a
  variety of ways from surveys to reordering).

The more different ways there are of measuring things (though
one may be key from the point of view of control) the more you
can ring the changes and extend the ways in which you can
highlight achievement in order to motivate. The more things
there are about which people can say 'That worked out well' or
'Did well there' the better. If a job does not obviously have such
points about it, then, if necessary, they must be sought out. The
job that allows people no opportunity to feel they have done

well will always be less satisfying. There is a danger here too. If there are no obvious achievement factors to focus on, then because people want them, they will invent them. This may be harmless, but it might put the emphasis on the wrong things to the detriment of more important issues. For example, people with repetitive tasks of some sort to do may focus on the volume – 'Another 20 done, great!' – rather than the quality of what they are doing.

The same principle applies informally where regular tangible measurements are less prescribed, so that simply saying things like 'Let's make that even more tomorrow' is important too. If tangible targets can be given then positive motivation makes it a good principle to 'aim high' – stretching people, who then find that when they do achieve, the feeling of achievement is that much more satisfying.

Achievement is the most powerful motivator, and therefore one of the most useful. What is more, its power is enhanced many times when it is linked to the next factor.

recognition

Achievement is important, people like it and it represents a major part of total job satisfaction. Beyond this, *recognition* of achievement is an even more vital part of good motivation. It also sits best with good management. Thus unless things are well organized, people know what to do and have clear objectives, achievement and its recognition may be difficult.

Recognition of achievement can be minor and momentary. For example, the simplest form is just saying 'Well done!' (And how many of us can put our hand on our heart and swear that we have done this as much as would have been useful over, say, the last month? Be honest.) A host of simple phrases combining recognition with encouragement are possible: 'Great job' – 'Excellent' – 'That's it'. Such phrases can be used to link into discussion: 'However did you manage that?' – 'Finished already?'

Alternatively, recognition can be major and tangible. For example: a salary increase (awarded for merit), a promotion or an incentive payment of some sort are all at the other end of the scale from a simple 'Well done', and there are a great many forms of motivation that come between these two extremes. The boxed text that follows extends the thinking about what one simple principle can prompt in terms of motivational action.

Extending the impact of recognition
Taking recognition of achievement as one area, let us start with 'Well done' and other simple acknowledgements. First it should be noted that such praise can be made progressively more powerful. For example, by:

- being said publicly (as during a departmental meeting) rather than in private;
- endorsed by someone senior, in writing or in person;
- noted in more widely visible form, in an internal newsletter or by being posted on the notice board (electronic or otherwise), for instance;
- repeated, for example a comment being made to someone as something happens, then forming part of a subsequent, more formal, discussion.

These examples are not, of course, mutually exclusive. Someone may sometimes do something that merits a whole range of responses, all in some way acknowledging what they have done with one acknowledgement reinforcing and adding power to the last. Other extensions of the 'Well done' include such things as:

- employee of the month schemes (with a public identification as in hotels);

> ■ certificates, badges, awards and even ties and tie-pins –
> anything that provides a visible reminder of what has
> been done;
> ■ informal tokens: going right through to giving a bunch
> of flowers or a meal or a drink (though it is, sadly
> perhaps, necessary to say that such gestures must be
> done in a way that cannot be misinterpreted. After all, if
> a thank you is seen as an unwelcome proposition, then
> it may do more harm than good).
>
> *Note:* This sort of action can be applied as much to groups as to
> individuals. Part of keeping in touch (and what some now call
> 'management by walking about') involves motivation. It is as
> useful on occasion to speak to a whole department as to one
> member of it. A 'Well done' may make a good start to a depart-
> mental meeting, for example, even if other topics are the reverse
> of praise. The only caveat here is that such praise must always be
> deserved; if it seems contrived then people will be puzzled (suspi-
> cious even) rather than being made to feel good.

recognition through rewards

The combination of recognition with achievement is an appropriate place to consider the whole question of tangible rewards:
that is everything from salary on that is part of the remuneration package. This includes:

■ *Company cars:* which certainly have a value. However,
it is important not to overlook the downsides, or make
unwarranted assumptions about their power. Tax has
risen dramatically on company cars (in the UK), and
they are apt to be taken as a right. Also, given the
emotive nature of the car itself promoted by the
automotive industry, they seem both to create
the possibility of dissatisfaction and to become time-
consuming. Companies are full of people trying to

buck the system – 'But, I want the soft top, and it can only be red' – 'The diesel, you are joking!?' – and, at worst, there are organizations where even the mention of the words 'company car' can turn whoever manages the scheme into a frustrated, blubbering wreck. Despite all this cars remain an important part of many a package and are inherently seen as a kind of recognition.

■ *Commission:* this is usually defined as payment, most often on top of salary, linked to results (as with sales commission). This will only be motivational if it is correctly set up. We return to this is Chapter 5, but briefly this means it must: be personal (team commission is possible, but has less effect in raising individual's motivation), have the payment linked directly to activity and results, and be easy to calculate. (The timescale must not be too long – something paid monthly is better than something paid quarterly, and annual commission quickly becomes viewed as a right and has a very limited motivational effect). In addition, and this almost goes without saying, it must be significant as a proportion of income. These days it is as well for managers to bear in mind their people's family income, because what is judged as significant will, for many, relate to a household in which both partners are earning. Remember too that there is a difference between what you might call commission (payment for past results) and an incentive (designed to boost future performance). Only payments that meet the criteria described will work as an incentive, and it is very easy for ill-judged schemes to become seen as a right or simply felt to be too insignificant or complex to be worth bothering about.

Commission or incentive 'payments' may be in other forms than money – gifts, theatre tickets... whatever. These need to be chosen to match what people want (and with care about tax implications); some may lend themselves to group activity or the involvement of people's partners – as with travel (an overseas conference is a good example). Incentive schemes such as competitions can be fun and work well, though remember that if the same person always wins, others will quickly lose interest. Regular, overlapping schemes – perhaps something different each quarter – can work well and can also be varied to keep up the level of interest they create.

■ *Financial assistance:* money talks, so this includes: rail season ticket loans, house or other loans at a special rate, and payment for things such as healthcare insurance, life insurance, travel insurance (covering personal/family travel as well as business trips), credit cards, etc. The mix of such benefits that a person gets is often public knowledge and a better package can be created as a recognition of good performance. There is also sometimes a trade off involved here between salary and these kinds of benefit. It may either be more valuable (or seen as more prestigious) for someone to have an additional benefit added to their package rather than a small salary increase, much of which goes in tax payments. This may be better for the individual, or the organization, or, indeed, sometimes both.

■ *Pensions:* a very important area these days (not least one affecting the original choice to take a particular job), with all the elements that make for a good pension potentially adding to its value. Pension benefits are sometimes less well appreciated among younger people, and will thus fail to be an attractive motivator. Advice plus pension benefits may thus persuade someone that there is something worthwhile on offer and do the person a long-term service as well. For some, however, this may illustrate that not everything you may judge 'worthwhile' instantly or equally appeals to others.

■ *Expenses:* these are payments that cover more than repaying monies spent on business (again watch the tax situation – for instance on things like petrol). For example, a credit card paid for by the employer may have a variety of money-saving advantages, such as providing free travel insurance, that save the recipient a worthwhile sum of money. Even seemingly small things such as the scheme some companies have allowing people to charge books bought to read on overseas flights and trips (provided they go back into the company library afterwards). This is a little thing, but can be much appreciated. Firm policy is necessary in this area or people will take advantage, costs will rise and elements of unfairness will intrude. I remember hearing someone bemoaning the fact that a charge for tennis lessons had been turned down when he had had to spend a weekend at a hotel in the Middle East, despite his pleas that 'there was nothing else to do'.

Note: another, slightly vexed, question concerns the rewards people may obtain from other perks: perks begetting perks, as it were. By this I mean things such as the results of airline (or other company) loyalty schemes. Does the free flight, once it is clocked up, belong to the employee or the company? Many, especially larger firms, leave it to the employee; but some clear policy may be necessary here (and perhaps an eye on the tax situation).

■ *Profit share, bonus or share schemes:* all these kinds of scheme can bind people to the organization and are used to link performance and payment. At senior level these can be not only very powerful, but also sometimes cause a clash of interest, with decisions about the organization in danger of being made on the basis of how they will affect people's pockets rather than to create the best situation for the firm. These schemes are now used successfully at every level, though professional guidance is recommended in their set-up so that tax and other details are well accommodated. Recognition comes into the picture if schemes are only available after, say, five years' service – they become a reward for service and performance during that time.

■ *Holidays:* these are important and link with family life (mentioned elsewhere). Both the length and choice of holiday dates and the way in which the organization operates around public holidays such as Christmas can be used motivationally (for example, in some organizations holidays increase – as may other perks – after a certain length of service). Logistics can be brought to bear also – for example, by allowing (encouraging?) someone making a business trip to link holiday to it if this makes a financial saving, allows a holiday in some interesting place, or both.

the work itself

We all spend a major part of our lives at work. So, unsurprisingly, it helps if people like the work they do. This means that some jobs are easier to motivate people in than others; they are inherently more interesting, worth while – or fun. But even if the work itself is dull, the workplace need not be; nor need what any particular work contributes to results be insignificant (there is a clear link here back to recognition).

In looking at your own staff, and in recruiting them too, you do need to think about round holes and square pegs. People who are in positions they are just not suited to will always be difficult to motivate, and may never produce the quality of work and productivity you want.

Bear in mind that other factors reviewed here influence this one. For instance, even dull work can be made more attractive if communication is good, if people know how they fit into the whole picture and see that their contribution is regarded as important and valued.

Many managers take steps to extend the scope of the work, adding or involving additional aspects that are there, in part, to motivate. Schemes such as quality circles, or simply a suggestions box, may add to people's perception of their job and produce something useful at the same time. As an example, I remember being collected from an airport by a hotel car whose driver exemplified this idea. Essentially he was a taxi driver, but he clearly saw his job as that of a scene-setter. His chatter on the way to the hotel informed, persuaded and made me look forward to the visit. It was done naturally and with great enthusiasm; and made a considerable impression. I bet it was more fun for him too to take this attitude than to just shut up and drive, producing a friendly response from guests (and larger tips?). A plethora of things come to mind that make the job easier, yet go beyond that, for example:

■ *Equipment*: things like a fax, laptop computer, mobile phone or pager which can be used privately and which lighten the load. The proliferation of such equipment in recent years makes this worth further comment. The amount and type of equipment can be increased progressively. Computers make a good example. Perhaps the job necessitates a PC on the desk, but a laptop may be provided as well (allowing private use, more choice on timing and other advantages which make its provision motivational). Perhaps this is then upgraded, additional training provided or the use of the laptop may be linked to an element of home-working. All this provides a series of motivational occasions, and has practical value too, with, say, a report being written quietly at home without interruption and thus in half the time that it might have taken in the office.

Note: computers are sometimes (often?) used to provide self-motivation. More than one person has been known to spend more time than they should sending personal e-mails, combing through the detail of some favourite Web site or simply playing computer games. Management may allow or turn a blind eye to a little of this, perhaps on the basis that clamping down would act demotivationally. The sheer range of possibilities here and the potential waste of time is such that more and more organizations are laying down policy about it. This seems reasonable but, human nature being what it is, it must be done with care. If it is not done fairly or if it seems too draconian, then it may cause problems. An area to watch for the future, perhaps.

■ *Functionality:* this is used in a sense that links very much to equipment, but adds a separate dimension. A good example is computer systems (and therefore software). You often hear people apologizing to others for the system they use – 'Sorry, Mr Customer, but the system will only work if I enter the account number.' When things work well productivity (or customers in the example) are not the only ones to benefit; staff do too. This may be a consideration when originating or updating certain systems.

■ *Convenience:* here we might include taxis home if you work late (also a safety measure), parking space, crèches or childcare provision.

■ *Time saving:* a canteen (which may also promote social contact), on-site facilities (a shop, hairdresser, travel agent, etc) all have role to play and may save people money too. Here they are flagged as gestures to the fact that it is recognized that people work hard and that efforts are made to balance this in various ways.

■ *Smoking or non-smoking policy:* (still a slightly thorny area, though the non-smokers seem to be winning) it is difficult to please everyone, perhaps the best that can be done is to ensure people feel that arrangements are fair and reasonable. In passing, it does seem to me that the unsavoury sight of groups of employees clustered around the front door of offices, puffing away in all weathers and littering the entrance with their debris, is hardly likely to motivate them or impress visitors such as customers.

■ *Other equipment designed to improve conditions:* the likes of air conditioning, fans (in hot weather) and heating (in cold), being able to open a window, good lighting and plants.

■ *Environment:* this is probably an inadequate word (atmosphere?) but it may lead us to concepts that are important. Numbers of things are clear: things seem better if we have sufficient space (both to work, to interact – or to get away from – others), comfortable seating and the occasional cup of coffee or tea. Other things are more complex. For example, good reception and meeting areas, and therefore the confidence of knowing that visitors (customers, say, or others) are impressed, reflect back on staff. Communications is influenced by environment also. I once worked in a rambling old building, the result of knocking two buildings together. Nothing fitted. Going between floors meant going up, and down and up again, cutting through several offices on the way. But it was comfortable; and it worked. Keeping in touch with others was no problem. Informal communications were excellent – you could not help but keep in touch. This easy and regular contact led to enhanced collaboration between people and to creativity. When the company moved to larger premises, things were better arranged – or so it seemed. In fact an important aspect of communication was lost and new measures were needed to compensate when this was recognized.

All these and more can be important. So too can the general atmosphere of the offices, and things like there being somewhere nice to meet with visitors. Other things will go hand in hand with particular jobs, everything from adequate filing space to little things like maybe a drum card index for someone who is constantly having to check telephone numbers or addresses.

Managers have to get into the nitty-gritty of other people's jobs in order to see the details that can influence motivation in these ways. It is easy to be distanced from this and thus miss the opportunity both to be seen to care and understand and to motivate by making a difference, though before moving on it should perhaps be noted that sometimes the management job is to explain that everything cannot be just as people would wish, with sufficiently good reason that demotivation is prevented. Now, back to positive influences.

responsibility

This goes hand in hand with the work involved. It can be exemplified by linking back to an earlier example. My hotel driver, using the journey to enthuse his passengers about the hotel to which they were going, was taking on more responsibility than just that of being a driver. As a result everyone gained. Most people enjoy responsibility – having something that is 'theirs'. They 'take ownership', to use current jargon, and put more into something as a result.

In one organization they found that simply requiring people in a clerical office to sign their own letters with their own name, instead of preparing everything for signature by a manager, brought an immediate increase in productivity and accuracy. People had responsibility, they somehow regarded it as more important to get it right than in the past.

There are links here to organization, work allocation and delegation. Giving people responsibility prompts their giving greater thought to their work and thus, very often, produces not only greater productivity, but is likely to improve efficiency, quality, indeed any measure that may be involved in being successful. Not least it can spark creativity. Managers who have a team of people should use them. You are not paid to sit and have all the ideas necessary to keep your department or whatever running efficiently, and then just tell people what to do. But you probably *are* paid to make sure there are *sufficient* ideas to make things work. No organization can remain the same, ideas are needed to fuel constant change and development.

Give people responsibility – ask – and you might be surprised how creative they can be. Perhaps there can only be one departmental manager, but there can surely be a host of subsidiary responsibilities, people in charge of projects, becoming your 'expert on...' (an industry, customer-type, IT development, etc), briefing newcomers, maintaining records or updating information and so on. And in every case this can potentially improve motivation and performance.

Projects – a key example
Projects get individuals involved, give them things to do – to think about, check out, investigate, study, suggest and so on – that become their projects, and can be referred to as such. Even something as simple as maintaining a departmental holiday chart might be used to give to a junior member of the team – better still one who likes and is good at doing such a thing neatly – the feeling of having something that is their responsibility. You will likely need a constant supply of such projects, overlapping, involving different people and linking, of course, to other areas such as training or innovation.

Note: strictly speaking it is rightly said that responsibility cannot be given, it can only be taken. You can provide the opportunity for others to take on responsibility, but it is up to the individual to make something of it. An ambitious individual, wanting responsibility, will probably work on their manager, actively seeking just such opportunities. More to the point here, the manager wanting to use the power of responsibility to motivate should bear this in mind. The process involves encouraging people to want it, helping them to seek it out and take it on – and providing feedback that oils the wheels and leads to people gaining from the process and getting things done also, much more than by just saying 'Do this' and hoping that people both do it well and are motivated by doing so.

advancement

No one likes to stand still. People like to feel they are making career progress. Indeed, because of what may go with it (a better salary, say) they may feel the need very strongly. But, that apart, the very feeling of making progress is motivational. Taking on additional small responsibilities may be part of that. So too is the way you organize and use the organizational hierarchy. Promotion is, of course, motivational. Grades and titles may be used to create sufficient levels so that people are able to rise and rise again. This may assist retention of good staff. It is in its way a form of recognizing achievement and it works well.

In Sales, for example, maybe there are four grades: Sales Executives, Senior Sales Executives, Account Managers and Key Account Managers; or more. In part such an arrangement may reflect the different jobs to be done, in part it may be to provide a number of steps up. In fact such divisions can often do both things. Stepping stones are provided, and the steps are, and are seen to be, real, and they link to salary and terms and conditions as well as job titles. If this principle is applied to parallel promotion ladders, then the incentive can be provided to remain on one where this is to the advantage of the company and the individual. Figure 4.1 illustrates this; the two ladders are best thought of as being related. One might be carrying out a specialist function (anything from working in a call centre to

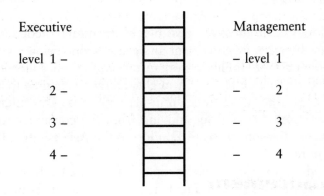

Figure 4.1 *Parallel promotion ladders (note: the relative levels of the two ladders can be varied)*

writing computer programs), the other is layers of management supervising the same area. This will help retain such specialist staff in their specialist areas and prevent the only means of advancement being changing roles (in this case to management, which requires very different skills).

Work at giving people something to aim at, regular changes and evidence of real progress and they will stay longer and work more effectively in a job than if they think they are in a rut. It is said there is all the difference in the world between five years' experience and one year's experience multiplied by five; and everyone wants the first of these. Job appraisals are important to motivation just because they relate directly to this area and thus provide a significant opportunity for management (more of this on page 108).

growth

Two kinds of progress are possible. Motivational theory differentiates between advancement and growth, one being progress within a current employer's organization, the other movement out and on to a better job. It might rightly be claimed that for large organizations there is an in-between area. This might be characterized by someone moving from the consumer to the industrial division, or from London to the Asia Pacific HQ in Singapore.

Good motivators make people leave. Really. It is not a contradiction – think about it. If no one ever left your team, what would it mean? Probably that people were all too mediocre to get better jobs; or even to try to do so. Of course, for the most part, people move on eventually. The trick is to build a first-class team (one whose members can ultimately get better jobs elsewhere if there are no internal promotion opportunities), but to retain them and maximize their performance as long and as much as possible.

For example, sometimes with high-calibre technical or sales staff, the industry norm is for fast turnover. In such a case just getting people to stay an average of, say, three years rather than two may be worth a considerable amount of money. If motivational action can achieve greater retention, then the time it takes to ensure this happens may be amply repaid.

the full mix

As with the negative factors reviewed in the preceding chapter, what is important here is the net effect of all the influences, and ultimately of the balance of all the positive and negative factors together. By balance is meant that the overall effect is positive, and sufficiently positive to hold and satisfy people. Some jobs have elements that weigh very heavily on one side or the other.

This can only be said with an individual in mind. Take travel as an example. An export job that had someone away more than at their desk, and criss-crossing the globe from one time zone to the next, might be regarded by some in very negative terms. Someone else, perhaps without family ties, might revel in it. Whoever is involved and whatever the mix of factors their job entails, the mix must work – or be made to work – for them. The way motivation works is thus progressive and cumulative. Every small factor may add a weight to one side of the positive/negative balance – in a way that ends up making the overall motivational climate what we want, and what our people want.

There are already many factors to consider here. Several main areas, for example, formal incentive schemes and communication, which have already been touched on here, will be explored in more detail later. Next we turn to how to measure the current motivational climate as a prerequisite to making improvements.

5

taking the temperature

At this point it should be clear that motivation matters and that motivational feeling results from a plethora of different factors; and that managing the mix means motivational feeling can be altered. So far so good, but if you plan to affect something it is a good idea to know what it is, not least so that you can know whether action taken has had some sort of effect or not.

Hence the need to take the temperature, as it were; that is to discover exactly how people feel. This is important both in a general 'people' sense, yet goes further; after all individuals are motivated and any measurement needs to probe to that level.

Motivation can be an area of some surprises. Signs may be misleading. Even when the signs are read correctly and action has been taken to improve motivation, there may seem to be no change. Timing is important. Attitudes usually indicate problems with motivation, before performance declines and makes it obvious that something is wrong, provided they are noticed. This means that the aware manager may be able to prevent performance decline before it occurs. But it also means that time must be given for solutions to work. An action taken may well begin to improve motivation before there are any signs of productivity or performance lifting.

If management is to be in a position to act promptly over motivational matters, then it must have a clear and accurate idea of what the motivational feeling is at any particular moment. The dangers of managers' perceptions lagging reality are obvious. Because of the problem of reading the signs (see Table 5.1), simply 'keeping an eye on things' may not be enough, and more formal measures need to be sought to obtain a more complete picture.

Table 5.1 *Problems with reading the signs*

Information may be omitted or disguised because of:

- people intentionally hiding their feelings;
- people's managers suggesting feelings should be hidden;
- office politics;
- fear of reprisal if forthright views are expressed;
- organizational culture (it is simply not done);
- desire to please;
- peer pressure;
- intended disruption, and therefore a wrong impression given;
- lack of understanding;
- lack of time;
- inadequate communications channels or opportunity and a feeling that whatever is said no one is listening.

There is merit in considering points such as these in the context of your own organization to see whether problems can be anticipated and prevented. Such thinking often needs to be repeated for different groups, and considered in the light of changing circumstances. For example, a group may be temporarily inclined to silence while they, say, sum up the likely attitude of a new manager. Or they may provide feedback in anger over some development which reflects the heat of the moment, rather than a considered view that emerges later

Though the merit of up-to-date and accurate information about motivational feelings may be clear, obtaining it needs some organization. However, if a systematic approach is adopted, then information can be updated regularly without a disproportionate expenditure of time. The dangers should be borne in mind. If a lack of information results in a lack of action, a small problem getting bigger, and a decline in performance, then the results can be far-reaching and costly. Time spent on this aspect of motivation, as on any other, provided it is well judged, is time well spent. So, how can you read the signs accurately?

accurate measurement

The case for good motivation is clear to most managers. Some have natural instincts for working with their staff to monitor and maintain a positive motivational climate. They seem to have a permanently 'hands-on' way of operating that always keeps their fingers on the pulse. Others have to work at even remembering to say 'Well done' sufficiently often, or may fail to recognize the need for action in this area or for particular manifestations of it.

If everyone is to have motivation sufficiently at the forefront of their mind for it to make a real difference to the way their people work, then action needs to be taken on a *regular* basis to ensure this happens. This need cause no great problem, as it can primarily be made possible by fitting approaches for building measurement of motivational feeling into certain activities that take place in the normal course of events. Beyond that, if more detailed information is necessary, then a larger thermometer as it were will be needed and other techniques may be called on. We will look at the overall task progressively, reviewing how the overall background strategy contributes, approaches to continuous measurement, making that measurement work and going beyond that if necessary.

creating a strategy to influence motivation

In an organization of any size there will be a number of managers. Only in the smallest company can everyone report to the same person. However, whomsoever a member of staff reports to, that person holds the prime responsibility for their motivational well-being. For line management motivation simply 'goes with the territory'. The effect will – indeed should – spill down through the hierarchy. Even the most caring and charismatic leader cannot do the whole job of motivating every employee; whatever other influence may help, it is the line manager's job to see that the net result is positive and rarely can this be done without him or her contributing to the process.

Whether something is taken as a given in an organization has come to be referred to as a cultural factor. We talk about organizations where the culture promotes service or quality excellence, or where training is seen as an inherent part of the foundation from which success can spring. Such initiatives – for they should be both intended and initiated – often stem from the top. That is not to say that influence cannot be brought to bear from elsewhere within the organization, but that is a difficult task if there is no contribution or support from higher up.

Creating an appropriate culture is a major task and may be linked to the broader area of the management of change (the details of which are beyond our brief here). Two factors are, however, worth a mention. Whether there is a culture that recognizes that motivating and all that goes with it is important will depend on both people and systems.

people

Many factors, starting with recruitment, can be instrumental in ensuring that managers are concerned about motivation. If this is the case, then there can develop a positive feedback loop that maintains the situation. Managers working at motivation create good feelings and good performance. This, in turn, is noticed, and more of the same gains acceptance because it is seen as keeping the process going.

In addition, certain people, not only in specialist areas such as personnel or training, may be in a position to act as champions for the motivational cause, as it were. Their role becomes to do more than motivate their direct subordinates, rather to promote any matter that seems to them likely to help motivation flourish more widely. They may be the one whose awareness allows them to raise and explain a potential problem before it does any damage, or who volunteer to take on tasks affecting the general good.

Senior management may well organize or encourage this. Such people may be recognized or may work in the background largely unnoticed, or at least without formal acknowledgement.

The more people devote time to motivation the better; every contribution counts, so what you do may have (or intend) implications beyond a particular section and this broader role may usefully be borne in mind. As just a small example, consider how you might influence the switchboard operator or receptionist. Everyone has contact with them. Maybe your contact can increase their motivational feeling and mean that they provide your section with exactly the service you want. Such must not be pursued to the exclusion of other priorities, of course, but doing so sufficiently to influence matters as may be beneficial is worth a thought, and some time.

systems

Systems can act (almost) independently of people to provide reminders and prompts to focus attention both on the specifics of motivation and on the idea that it is an important responsibility. Some examples will quickly illustrate the possibilities:

■ Interviewing procedures can be arranged so that potential new managers' attitudes to motivation are checked out as part of the recruitment process.

■ Managers' job descriptions must specifically make clear their role as motivators.

■ Remuneration policy should be checked regularly and adapted as necessary.

■ Communications that are an inherent part of corporate working must be seen as having motivational constituents (eg avoiding unnecessary secrecy and scotching inaccurate rumours).

■ Communications methods that assist motivation must be in place (eg everything from a company newsletter or magazine to a notice board).

■ Social activity may need to be instigated (and maintained) as part of a motivational strategy (eg sports clubs).

■ Appraisal processes – from the forms used to the interviews the process uses – must consider motivational influences as one factor determining the configuration they take.

■ Policies on matters such as absenteeism or discipline must also be constructed with motivation in mind.

■ Specific motivational schemes organized on a company-wide basis (eg employee of the month) will help focus attention on the process.

You may not be able to influence everything on such a list, but whatever the position in which you work in your organization you should be able to assist to a degree. A checklist of systems may be worth reviewing within a specific organization to see how well systems accommodate the motivational implications inherent in them. For example, something as simple as installing a staff notice board not only provides a new means of possible motivation, and extends communication with employees, but provides a way to prompt managers to take that particular initiative. Similarly, tightening a policy on, say, absenteeism might itself increase hours worked and improve motivation in a hard-working group with a dislike for 'passengers'. Surely almost anyone might instigate such things (even if the sanction of others is required to complete the process). Both people and systems can have an ongoing influence on how well the need for motivational activity, and thus logically the measurement of current motivation, is accepted – and thus on how effectively it is carried out.

approaches to continuous measurement

Unlike the next two stages, here we consider things that are unashamedly informal, though there is nevertheless real merit in approaching them systematically. A little considered effort here can reduce the need for some of the more formal approaches that can improve the perception of just what current motivational feelings are like. Continuous measurement comes down to little more than the need for all managers to keep an ear to the ground; though the ear and the mind behind it must be open.

Actually if informal checking is viewed this simplistically then insufficient justice may be done to it. Much of what is involved is encapsulated in a phrase that was, I think, originated in the classic book *In Search of Excellence* (written by Tom Peters and Robert Waterman: Harper & Row: 1982). Abbreviated to MBWA, the phrase was Management By Walking About. They made the very good point that many managers might perform less well than they might simply because they were out of touch with people. The more people you have to keep in touch with, the easier it is to find yourself with this problem.

This principle is certainly true of motivation. Managers will never know how people feel if they never meet them. There is no substitute for personal experience, and even the best-briefed subordinates, for all the walking about they may do on managers' behalf, can only report back second-hand.

So, the key technique here is to meet people. Managers must visit the people who make up their organization, going right through the hierarchy and yet doing so in a way that does not give a patronizing impression. If the 'boss' is seen to descend from on high, as it were, very occasionally and for a matter of moments, this may be less than useful and may even be actively resented. If managers develop the habit of 'walking about', giving sufficient time to it and spending real time with individuals – and showing real interest – then they may genuinely build up an accurate picture of how people feel about things (and collect some interesting ideas along the way). While the size of an organization may preclude senior managers communicating face-to-face with everyone, careful judgement of who and how many people are seen, and where they sit in the hierarchy of the organization, is both necessary and worthwhile.

Rather than leaving this thought simply as an intention to be commended, it is worth making a number of points about what makes such a process productive. Certainly certain mixing can be formalized. In some organizations this occurs through specific kinds of meeting. For example, a product briefing meeting for sales or customer support staff might usefully be attended by someone from another department. Perhaps this could be from Production or Research and Development. One opportunity (among others) of such occasions is a measurement of motivation.

More important, management needs to allocate some time for informal checking. This should in part be general, but also via particular individuals. Indeed, for employees down the line simply having a busy manager showing an interest in them may itself be motivational, so measurement and influence can go arm in arm. Such contact, as goes almost without saying, is only going to be motivational if the interest shown is felt to be genuine. In the larger organization this makes such things as remembering people's names very important. Around and about the organization, whatever the scale on which it is useful for you to do so, the key intentions of MBWA should be to:

- *Observe:* keep your eyes and ears open and take in (and note, later perhaps) what is picked up. Some excursions can have a specific chosen intention and agenda, such as to ascertain the attitudes to a recent change. Others may be more general.
- *Encourage feedback:* if contacts are seen to have purpose (and this may be primarily operational) then people may quickly get into the habit of giving their views and ideas. If they can be encouraged to speak out, openly and honestly, and constructively, then little more may be necessary.
- *Ask (and listen):* general encouragement is good; specific questioning may be better. Here it is important that questions create genuine dialogue rather than a monologue. Two things are key here. First, that a manager does not influence the opinions given, for example by saying something like: 'The reorganization seems to be working well, moving dispatch and order processing in together was a good idea – what do you think?' Such phrasing will guarantee some people do no more than agree, whatever their real feelings may be. Secondly, questions need to get people talking. Few closed questions (which can prompt only 'Yes' or 'No' answers), more open questions – what, why, when, where, how and who – that get people talking. Starting with 'Tell me about...' works well; and if necessary 'Tell me *more* about...' will help dig deeper.

  Beyond that it is essential to listen, really listen, to what is said in reply. Listening must be an active process – see the checklist in Table 5.2.

Table 5.2 *Active listening*

The following will help ensure that maximum useful information is gathered quickly and in a way acceptable to others:

- *Want to listen* – knowing it is necessary is the first step.
- *Look like a good listener* – people will be more forthcoming if they believe the questioner is interested.
- *'Read between the lines'* – there is more to be learned than just what the words say.
- *Stop talking* – no one can talk and listen properly at once.
- *Use empathy* – putting oneself in others' shoes is appreciated and helps create rapport.
- *Check* – clarify as necessary (some people may have useful information but put it without great clarity).
- *Remain unemotional* – save most responses until later and concentrate on fact-finding.
- *Concentrate* – allow nothing to distract you.
- *Look at people* – eye contact breeds trust and creates the right atmosphere.
- *Note key points* – though not necessarily by scribbling them down as people say them.
- *Avoid personalities* – listen to what is said, rather than letting who says it colour the first view of it.
- *Avoid arguments* – gripes may occur, but it may not be appropriate to deal with them there and then.
- *Avoid negatives* – concentrate on the positive in how things are put across (not 'Tell me about the problems', but rather 'How do you think this can be improved?').
- *Make notes* – time should be allowed as part of the exercise (and after the conversation) to note down impressions gained, consolidate them and begin to draw conclusions.
- *Test* – finally, always test the information collected. One person expressing a view does not automatically mean everyone thinks the same; neither does it mean no one else shares the view. MBWA is valuable not just in obtaining information, but in identifying areas that need more – and perhaps more formal – investigation, or verification.

Habit is a key word here. Managers who begin to spend time in this way will usually report that it is useful, and this fact helps ensure that they do so on a regular basis, which in turn can lead to it becoming a habit. All the information gleaned in this way creates a foundation of knowledge about motivation that can be added, or filled out, by any more formal action that is taken.

specific measurement opportunities

In addition to the ongoing measurement referred to above, it is clearly helpful if there are specific instances and events which can be utilized in the cause of measuring motivational levels. Any occasion on which this can happen can help guarantee that measurement takes place, and that the amount of measuring going on is sufficient to produce a useful picture. Clearly it is easier for managers to utilize existing activity rather than seek to introduce additional tasks which may, at the time, seem less than essential.

The first job is therefore to ascertain whether such occasions exist. Some will be common to most managers, and others will apply only to those in certain jobs. Two key occasions, which are used here as examples, are: the regular appraisal meetings which most staff participate in; and so-called 'exit interviews' which are held in many companies with individuals just prior to their leaving to take up employment elsewhere.

The checklist in Table 5.3 shows a number of examples of events that can be used in this way. It is a useful exercise to see how many occasions like these can be identified and made use of in a particular organization, indeed among a particular group of staff. The examples given are necessarily general. The particular activities of staff may prompt further opportunities, say involving technical briefings.

Table 5.3 *Measurement occasions: examples*

- ▦ appraisals (annual meetings and other periodic appraisal sessions);
- ▦ exit interviews;
- ▦ project meetings;
- ▦ departmental meetings;
- ▦ individual counselling sessions;
- ▦ discipline meetings;
- ▦ evaluation of group training activities and courses;
- ▦ briefing or one to one training sessions;
- ▦ informal meetings (from lunch to crossing on the stairs).

What is being suggested is that regular interaction with staff on such occasions cannot be made to achieve only the prime purpose, but also plays a part in the necessary motivational measurement. Some of the above, for example training evaluation processes, are inherently, in part, concerned with checking motivation. Others are primarily for other purposes. More details of three of these, training assessment, job appraisal and exit interviews, are given in Chapter 7 in the context of communication.

major measurement

A major overall technique designed specifically to measure employee motivation is that of employee opinion polling. Used regularly in some organizations, it can also be a useful one-off measure at times when the information it produces is particularly necessary and perhaps urgent. Examples of such circumstances include the appointment of new senior managers who have no experience of the staff, or organization takeover, reorganization or merger that creates situations where the views of staff may be urgently needed. There is no reason, however, why the principles involved cannot be used in simple form with quite small groups of people.

This technique is, as the name suggests, a close relative of formal research techniques used to do market research, or discover political views and voting intentions. It is thus something used at a distance, as it were, and in a way that announces its intention openly. While some of the informal checking used as measurement does not need to be flagged as specifically 'checking your motivation', this does. It is thus best used when there is a clear reason for such a check, and also when the reason – though it may need explaining – is certain to be understood by staff.

Like research, if large numbers of people are to be involved, as in a large organization, then it is possible to take a representative sample of people rather than polling everyone. Note that what constitutes a statistically valid sample needs identifying precisely; this may be an area for expert advice, as may other aspects of the pure research techniques involved here (guidelines on best practice in employee research published by the UK Market Research Society may be a useful reference).

Polls can be intentionally timed ahead of a change, perhaps to produce 'benchmark' information at that point. Or they can be conducted after a change; or both. In all such cases their remit may be broad. Alternatively, they may have a particular focus. For instance it may be useful to check employee opinions about a new development (say, a new product, or a new way of working), or about customer relations (ranging from their perception of service to technical use of a product). As with so much else in corporate life, clear objectives are an essential ingredient of success, indeed the whole process must be approached systematically, through the steps that follow.

creating an environment that will allow a poll to succeed

The origination of an employee opinion poll needs careful consideration. The danger is that the very fact of a poll being conducted will be seen as an admission of failure or difficulty, even when it is designed to prevent problems or to take an existing situation forward. Two preconditions are important to its acceptance: first, that it is championed. This means that it is seen as being initiated by someone (who might be a functional head or even the chief executive) with a valid motive and with commitment to making it work and the clout to see it through. If it is seen as just a 'good idea' or the pet project of someone in the bowels of Personnel then its rationale will be more difficult to sell. Secondly, it must be organized so as to make possible the gathering of genuinely open information. Opinion polls are to tell you what people *really* think. Only if people are *completely certain* that they can speak out without fear of comebacks will they do so.

The second point above means that it is virtually impossible to undertake an opinion poll, and create the necessary confidence in its confidentiality, without involving an outside agency. This may be a research company or consultancy of some sort; in either case what is most important is the perceived objectivity. Thus if a merger, say, makes polling the entire staff of an organization necessary, then an outsider with the resources to administer and analyse the large number of questionnaires involved may make sense. If the task is smaller and well within the capacities of a single consultant, then costs need not be high. Perhaps the most important criterion is that staff whose opinions will be sought do not see there being any unpleasant vested interest lurking at the back of the project.

communication

The methodology needs to be worked out and communicated clearly. Such communication should specify:

■ *The objective.* Why the poll is to be conducted should be clear, and the more specifically this is stated the better. There is a considerable difference between a project that is described as being 'just a check to see how people feel about the company', and one that is stated as being 'to provide feedback on people's current feelings, to ensure that the projected changes are carried through in a way that will enhance people's job satisfaction and avoid problems'. In the latter case, provided there is a link to a specific planned (and announced) change, the chances of people assisting the project are much greater.

■ *The methodology.* Staff need to be told exactly how information will be collected. An assurance of confidentiality needs to be clearly given. Small details may be important – for example, if a questionnaire is to be used, how long is it and how long will it take to complete (even whether this is to be done in private time or in the firm's time may be important to some employees).

■ *The reporting back procedure.* Spell out how long this will take, who will see what, in what form and any other appropriate details.

■ *The link to action.* It should be made clear that what is being done is not 'producing information for information's sake', but that it is a route to improvements. The more that can be said about that up front the better.

■ *Any exclusions.* A poll cannot be a cure-all, and must not be seen as such. It may help the future acceptance of findings and of actions that may follow if any areas that will specifically not be addressed as a result are noted (perhaps in some cases how they will be addressed can be added).

■ *Overall timing.* An advance announcement should spell out the full timing – when it will be done, how long it will take and when the findings – and action – may be expected thereafter.

methodology

Leaving the areas of information on one side for a moment, the canvassing of any number of staff needs to be efficiently set up and handled. The checklist in Table 5.4 highlights the key issues involved in ensuring the success of such an exercise.

Table 5.4   *Checklist: making polling successful*

The following should be born in mind:

- ■ Confidentiality needs to be stressed throughout the project.
- ■ Questionnaires should be clearly anonymous and without any codes that might seem to provide identification.
- ■ Questionnaires should be quick and easy to complete (eg ticking boxes rather than writing essays).
- ■ In order to double check that a questionnaire is effective, it may be useful to 'pilot' it – ie use it first on a limited basis to test it.
- ■ Questions should be carefully worded and unambiguous. (*Note:* care should be taken to make sure that questions do not act in a leading manner. For example, if a political pollster asked: 'Would you pay more in tax if this guaranteed less congestion on the roads?', this would perhaps prompt a different answer from the question: 'How important would you rate the need to reduce the congestion on the roads?' Or: 'Do you think more taxes should be levied from road use?' Similarly, if a question incorporates an opinion ('Prompt service to customers is very important, do you agree: very strongly, strongly, etc') rather than positioning its content without any pre-judgement ('How highly would you rate prompt customer service?' etc), then the latter is surely more likely to produce useful, rather than biased, information.)
- ■ Providing information should be strictly voluntary (though all the communication about the project should be such as to persuade most people to *want* to participate).

Table 5.4 *(cont'd)*

- ■ Any unions or staff organizations should be consulted and kept informed, and this is best started at an early stage (ahead of any action).
- ■ Time to complete the questionnaire should be provided (ie rather than requesting it back 'at the end of the week' or whatever, it may be better to pull people away from work and give them a set time to complete the information), though it may well be best to issue it in advance so that there is time to study or discuss it.
- ■ A ballot-box-type collection process may be useful to emphasize confidentiality.
- ■ Resources must be in place to see the project through and to do so on time; nothing creates a lack of credibility faster than saying that views will be canvassed, and that they will influence action, and then nothing happens – or nothing happens for too long.
- ■ Consider using other communications methods alongside the project communication to reinforce the impact (eg an internal newsletter or company magazine could report progress to date or give out certain advance findings).

interviews

Findings may be investigated further to explore in depth or more widely by using individual interviews. People must be selected carefully for this. A sample of the full group of employees being canvassed may be chosen, and this might be done at random (taking perhaps 10–15 per cent of the total group being canvassed). Alternatively, the full group can be used to identify the subgroup required for individual interview; or everyone can be interviewed if this is useful.

Selection of interviewees would be achieved by asking – perhaps as one of the questionnaire questions – for nominations of people the respondent feels will give a representative view on behalf of a group of employees. Then either individuals can be chosen at random from those listed, or a weighting factor can be introduced, for instance by asking for several nominations and then selecting those whose names crop up most frequently.

It should be noted that this aspect of the poll should, like the rest, be voluntary. Some people so selected may opt not to go for interview. The fact that the objectives have been clearly explained and that the interviewer is not a member of the organization's management will help ensure such fallout is minimal.

feedback

Analysis should be conducted promptly (at worst long delays will be interpreted as doctoring the findings). And the findings need to be published in full; if necessary this means warts and all. Omitting any aspect of the coverage of questions asked is dangerous. Employees will always put the worst interpretation on why answers to certain questions are not included (probably exaggerating any problem).

Often the kind of staff involved are not familiar with reports setting out a mass of figures, so make sure that the presentation of the findings is easy to read. The answers to main questions, most often selecting some form of rating, can best be set out in graphic form. See Figure 5.1, which shows a simple pie chart.

the areas questioned

There can be no universal standard poll questionnaire. Questioning must reflect the organization and the jobs and responsibilities of those to be polled. In a particular organization it may be possible to use one questionnaire to get a general idea of feelings around a wide workforce. However, if the polling is focused on one category of staff, or even one department, then more specific questions are possible, and more tailoring of the format will be necessary.

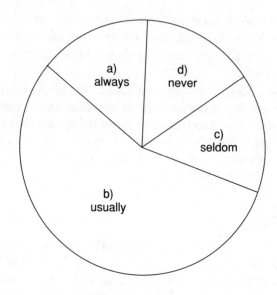

Figure 5.1 *Presenting findings*

Question: *My manager sets realistic targets: a) always, b) usually, c) seldom, d) never.*

The example in Table 5.5 shows a checklist of information that is designed to act as the first stage to preparing a tailor-made questionnaire for one specific staff group.

Note: rating scales used can be made most pointed when respondents are asked to select from an even number of options. This removes the option of a middle point – the ubiquitous average – and thus tends to produce more action-oriented information. If the intention is to provide a basis for action then this is surely better. Thus questions might ask respondents to tick whether something happens: never/seldom/usually/always. Or whether something is regarded as being: very useful/quite useful/not very useful/useless. And so on, depending on the topic of the question.

Table 5.5 *Checklist: compiling a poll questionnaire*

The following takes as an example one specific category of staff – in this case members of a field sales team – to show how question areas can be selected, and how specific questions can focus on the particulars of the role and tasks involved. So question areas might include the following (shown with some examples of the detailed areas that might be explored within each):

- The product range sold
    - How easy are they to sell?
    - How are they rated by customers?
    - How are they positioned alongside competitive products (or services)?
- The customers dealt with
    - What is their attitude to the organization and to the sales team?
    - How do they rate the service they receive?
    - What would make them increase business with us?
- Support provided
    - Are requests for support (on behalf of customers) promptly and efficiently dealt with?
    - Is information, and sales aids, provided by the organization relevant and useful?
    - Are sales meetings held constructive and useful?
- Relationships with others around the organization
    - How are relationships with other departments (eg technical or marketing) rated?
    - Are communications channels with others internally satisfactory?
    - Does action taken by others strengthen the sales relationship with customers?
- Career opportunities
    - Do people see career opportunities as a reason to stay with the organization?
    - Are longer-term career issues discussed?
    - How does this organization seem to rate with other potential employers?

Table 5.5   *(cont'd)*

■ Supervision
  - How is the respondent's immediate line manager rated (as someone to work for)?
  - Are objectives clearly spelt out and targets set sensibly and fairly?
  - Is contact and communications with the supervisor satisfactory and supportive?
■ Rewards
  - What are attitudes to salary?
  - How is the total package regarded (including incentives linked to performance)?
  - What changes would be appreciated?
■ Team working
  - How effectively does the team work together?
  - Does competition within the team help or hinder the achievement of planned results?
  - Are there any areas that give rise to friction among the group?
■ Work conditions
  - Are travel or time away from home intrusive or unreasonable?
  - What attitude is there to the required reporting systems?
  - Are there particular factors (eg company cars) about which there are suggestions or complaints?
■ Training and development
  - Do people feel the right training is provided and if so, is it sufficient?
  - Are there fears for the future about skills falling behind the needs of the market?
  - Do people see their job as something repetitive or as something that expands in scope over time?
■ Personal details
  - As questionnaires are anonymous it may be useful to collect some basic personal information to help position and analyse the answers given.
  - What age bracket are people in?
  - How long have they worked for the company?
  - Are they male or female?

The next example is included to show how quick checks can be made, precisely yet simply, to identify the feelings of a particular group of staff. Market Research Solutions Limited of Oxford not only conduct this sort of research for clients, but use it on themselves. One such use is to find out the feelings of the many freelance researchers who make up their total team. The whole questionnaire is not shown, though it is only three pages long. It asks some simple questions about such matters as the amount of work done for MRSL and the length of time a respondent has worked in the field, before asking for a list of comments designed to measure how working with MRSL is rated and how it compares with other firms the freelance might also work for on occasion. This list is shown in Table 5.6.

Table 5.6   *Freelance research staff questionnaire*

The list below is an extract from the questionnaire used by Market Research Solutions Limited to check the feelings of their own staff. The question asks: Using the ratings below, please tell us how MRSL compares with other companies you work for on each of the factors listed. Please circle only one code per statement, choosing the one that best reflects MRSL's overall position. The rating choices are: Best/Better/Average/Worse/Worst. The factors asked are:

- offers a good variety of work;
- gives good-quality instructions;
- pays promptly;
- offers fair rates of pay;
- is strict about field dates;
- is more relaxed about field dates;
- tries to give me the type of work I prefer;
- is old fashioned;
- gets the best out of the interviewers;
- gives unclear instructions;
- changes the nature of the work once I've agreed to do it;
- is trustworthy;

Table 5.6 *(cont'd)*

- ■ pays good attention to detail, rarely issues corrections;
- ■ handles pay invoices accurately;
- ■ delivers work in time for me to understand what is needed;
- ■ is well organized for returning work;
- ■ keeps me on my toes;
- ■ sends out questionnaires that are easy to follow;
- ■ is high tech;
- ■ treats me fairly;
- ■ has knowledgeable regional/area managers;
- ■ has knowledgeable field office staff.

Comparisons are sought in subsequent questions with specific other research companies. The way such a range of questions is used to build up a picture is well illustrated by this approach, as also is the potential manageability of such an investigation.

This makes a good example of manageability and focus, highlighting just how specific such measurement can be. Here the intention is clearly to promote good relations with people who are not full-time employees and therefore not easy to control, yet who are very important to the company's success and to the productivity of particular projects. Thanks to MRSL for permission to include this example here.

Of course, employee opinion polls may be much more extensive than this, as the checklist example shown in Table 5.5 shows. Always there needs to be a balance between the desire for greater amounts of information and the need to keep the process manageable, not least in the eyes of those who are asked to complete questionnaires, which should always be made easy to complete.

To add one small point: it may be useful sometimes to include a number of questions designed to gain opinions about the polling exercise itself. This is especially true if it is being done for the first time or if it links to sensitive issues (eg company reorganization).

The overall concept of employee opinion polling can be approached in a variety of ways. It can be an exercise in 'testing the water', perhaps linked to particular events or circumstances. Or it can be part of a more all-embracing strategy to this area. Overall, employee opinion polling provides a major means of checking motivational levels. It allows specific measurement linked to topical circumstances, or simply a judicious look at how things are linked to longer-term vision of the organization and its well-being. Even if this is something you use rarely, the principles involved are worth bearing in mind.

the link between information and action

It may be satisfying to have a clear idea of the motivational situation affecting a group of staff at any particular time (however that information has been acquired), but doing so should be regarded not as an end in itself but as a means to an end. If performance is significantly affected by people's prevailing state of mind, and it is, then action is the keynote here and, as was said early on, no one all-pervading action will set motivation firmly on the heights – it needs attention to detail.

As we have seen, information is available from a number of sources. Specifically these involve:

- informal *observation*: the continual assimilation of information from day-to-day management activities;
- directed *observation*: planned observation from specific activities that come to be habitually regarded as providing some part of the total information;
- dedicated *polling*: specific projects to 'take the motivational temperature'.

The total amount of information can be considerable, and of course is constantly changing in nature. In order that this does not become unmanageable it needs to be approached systematically. The details matter. Somewhere among the data there may be one or more particular factors on which action can, perhaps simply, lead to improved performance. In addition it is the overall conclusions drawn that lead to action on a broader front, and perhaps involving numbers of people, which can also influence the situation. The evidence, for that is what this information is, needs considering in a way that answers the following questions:

- Is the information safely recorded? The amount of detail involved makes it easy to miss out what may be important elements.)
- Is the information valid and reliable? (Or is more checking or the locating of supporting views necessary?)
- How should the information be rated? (In other words what elements are of greater or lesser importance?)
- Who, exactly, does the information relate to? (It can be dangerous to assume that what one person or group says applies equally or in the same way to others.)
- What are the time implications of particular factors? (Some things are perennial issues, others are linked to short-term or topical factors.)
- Do we accept the information? (This applies not simply to, say, the truthfulness of a view expressed, but to our allowing its credibility – it is all too easy to be censorious, feeling that because something would not worry us, it cannot be worrying others.)
- What are the priorities for action? (This differs from the rating above: for instance, something may be of minor importance but lend itself to immediate action, or of major importance but not able to be influenced at the present time.)

- ■ Does the information need consolidating? (ie Are there a variety of signs all stemming from one factor that can be grouped and dealt with as one issue?)
- ■ Is the information in a form that links to practical steps being taken? (There is little use in a mass of information if it cannot help us towards action.)

It should be noted that the reason for collecting information and seeing it as a springboard for action is twofold. First, if motivation is low then correcting action may be necessary. Secondly, and this is just as important, the information may explain *why* motivation is high, thus providing a basis to continue the situation or apply similar inputs to other situations.

A final point: all this links with what was said earlier about motivation taking time. It is necessary to go through the checks and information-gathering, and to spend time sorting and analysing the information that is collected in order that appropriate action can be taken. Some signs stand out individually. There is something obviously having a negative effect, say, and it is possible to fix on this, take corrective action and see an improvement result. But not everything will act alone or be so easy to see; the situation may well be complex and thus only open to real influence after due consideration.

a firm foundation

Certainly everything that you may do in motivation is likely to work better if you have a clear idea how people feel at any particular moment; and that demands some form of *regular* checking, however formal or informal that may be. This provides a firm foundation for action.

incentive schemes

Some of what needs to be done in motivation can be accomplished through formal incentive schemes. This phrase encompasses everything from annual bonuses to the payment of commission or the conduct of competitions with prizes in the form of merchandise or gifts.

a caveat

An important point needs making right at the beginning of any discussion of incentive schemes. *They are not a panacea.* It is vital that any such scheme is *not* considered either as the solution to all motivational problems, or regarded as meaning that other inputs, particularly those demanding management time, are unnecessary. If a chosen scheme is seen not only as a panacea, but also as the sole thing it is necessary to do, motivation may suffer badly.

Formal incentive schemes may well have a part to play, but it must be regarded as a part and not only must any scheme used suit well in its own right, it must also fit in with the other activities being actioned to create a suitable mix. Indeed, its use must be integrated with, and augmented by, a whole range of other activities; at its simplest this means that the recipient of an award coming from an incentive scheme feels even better about it if someone takes time to say 'Well done' too. As has been said already, no one action can create all the positive motivational input you want. The danger is that schemes are sometimes regarded in this way and other action goes by default. It is experience of this attitude that makes it sensible to put real emphasis on this warning. Enough. Let us turn to examine how any formal scheme can help.

employee packages

People do not work for just a wage or salary. There is usually a whole remuneration package and this should be assembled primarily with motivational intentions. The job of the package has two overriding intentions: first, to attract the right candidates to the job in the first place and allow successful recruitment and selection to take place. Attracting good candidates is a competitive process. In many job areas people have a choice – certainly good people – and they will only be attracted to your organization as a result of weighing up the pros and cons of what you offer alongside other prospective employers.

The second intention is to retain people in the job (at least while you want to do so!) and encourage them to remain with your organization, even if ultimately they move on to other than their original positions.

The elements of a package are many and varied, and include:

- salary;
- pension;
- company car;
- incentive or bonus payments;
- share options;
- special-terms loans;

- ■ expenses (that do more than cover the costs incurred on business);
- ■ discounts on company products or services;
- ■ health and other insurance;
- ■ group incentives (such as attending an overseas conference).

Not all of these are relevant to every organization. For example, your product may not be something an individual wants to buy, so special terms would be of no value. Otherwise all these can be used for motivational purposes.

It is possible, for example, to produce a mix that fits an individual's circumstances, and which perhaps boosts one element of the mix without taking the costs of the total package above what is reasonable. For instance, the cost of good secretarial staff has risen over the years, and good ones, especially in a city like London, are hard to find and difficult to retain. More than one manager I know has solved this problem by giving a senior secretary a company car (albeit a small one). This is unusual, and, matched to the needs of the individual, made the package so attractive that retention was secured long term with all the subsequent advantages.

A whole range of tricks can be used in this area to enhance the motivational value of elements of the package. Further examples are:

- ■ providing choice in an area such as a company car;
- ■ allowing health care insurance (now very much a given in many jobs) to cover the employee's family;
- ■ using an annual travel insurance policy (obviously for employees who need one for their work) that also covers holidays and family members;
- ■ granting loans for specific purposes, such as an annual season ticket for travel to work, which is of practical value to employees and saves them money.

It is worth keeping the 'standard' package under review and, while the mix must be seen to be fair to all, flexibility must be inherent to allow you to maximize the usefulness of any individual's package to them. While rules are important, real exceptions may be much appreciated, cost little yet still enhance the effect gained. As an example of a real departure from the 'standard mix' I remember a (single) colleague of mine being posted from London to Singapore for three years. The standard package included a company car. He knew Singapore. It is small, just a city, public transportation is excellent (for example, taxis are cheap and plentiful) and cars are taxed to make them *very* expensive. He asked if he could have a company motorbike. It gave him individual mobility when he needed it, the rest of the time he would use a taxi. Unusual, but the cost was small – the company gave him the bike, and they shared the saving: he got a higher salary and the company saved money on the overall deal.

Such things are motivational in two ways. First, it is appreciated that the company is flexible and that an individual arrangement is permitted. Secondly, the exception made is itself motivational. Both employee and employer win in such a case. The package forms the foundation to the way people are rewarded and how that reward is seen. Incentives go beyond this, however.

financial incentives

The problem with financial incentives is similar to that mentioned earlier about salary; it is quickly taken for granted and ceases actively to motivate. On the other hand, money is a great motivator, and how it is applied makes a difference. For example, certain jobs – perhaps sales is the best example – lend themselves to the payment of commission. The research done in this area provides valuable guidelines which can be applied more broadly. It shows that commission payment schemes work best when:

- they are a part, albeit a significant part, of a package that includes salary (commission only may work best, but only with certain kinds of people, those prepared to take that risk, and only if the job lends itself to it);
- they are wholly, or certainly primarily, individual (group incentives, where one person is dependent on the efforts of others, are always less powerful motivators);
- they allow regular payment (monthly, maybe quarterly, but leave it longer and people are distanced from it and it achieves less);
- The scheme is simple. It must be possible to work out how things are going and have a good idea what payment may be coming at the end of the period involved.

Any reversal of these principles – a complex group scheme that pays an annual bonus – is destined to cost more than it achieves. There is all the difference in the world between a package and payments, in whatever mix, that reward people and do so to their satisfaction, and payments designed to focus people's minds on their efforts. Incentives must be just that.

Payments in money are not the only option and a wide variety of other methods is available. This can be useful. If schemes are bought in, then the providers will often contribute to the overall process, perhaps providing help with communicating the scheme that makes it sound fun, interesting and attractive to all concerned. Many retailers operate schemes in which vouchers are paid out and can be cashed in by staff for goods. Other schemes are operated by specialist agencies, and may provide more choice that going to a single supplier. The specialists will, of course, claim that their offering works especially well, indeed some – travel is an example – are well proven, though nothing is guaranteed to have a universal appeal. An important caveat here is to remember the people involved – who is it that you want to motivate and what is likely to do so for them?

The need to avoid being censorious has been mentioned. Here the reverse is the worst danger. A scheme organizer may offer something that is attractively arranged, which seems cost-effective and which is grabbed at despite the fact that the basis is just something unlikely to appeal to the people concerned. Either their situation is not sufficiently thought about or something that appeals to the manager is arranged on the basis that 'people are bound to like it'. Some objective thought, even some research, is important here.

Nor do schemes of this sort have to be the only thing done. Within a chosen mix, a scheme may play a larger or smaller part. A mix is almost always best, and a prescribed scheme may be an important part of it; the danger is that because elements of the process can be delegated (for instance to a scheme organizer) the temptation is to allow it to undertake more of the job than is reasonable.

non-financial schemes

Other schemes may similarly work towards regular incentive payments, with these being paid in forms other than money. Travel is a well-known one, and a seemingly approved option, but all sorts of merchandise can be involved – you name it and someone will have linked it to an incentive scheme. Sometimes routine things are selected, sometimes something novel. Whatever it is must match the people involved (it is no good for a manager who is a keen gardener to use plant vouchers, say, for a spring scheme if all the staff concerned live in apartments).

Sometimes novelty is right; for example more than one company pays the first layout on their incentive scheme in the form of a down payment on a Rolls Royce. The incentive continues – you have to do well enough for subsequent payments to be made; or the car goes back!

tax implications

In the United Kingdom, at least, most payments made as part of a remuneration package, whether they represent an incentive or not, are taxable. The last thing you want is for this to dilute the effectiveness of such payments. There are two main levels of danger here. The first is that people may literally be caught out by this. They go off for what proves a lovely holiday, say – all expenses paid – return highly motivated, but some months later suddenly discover that there is a related tax bill to pay. Secondly, the fact of tax to pay, even if this is pointed out, seems to negate the advantage. The value of whatever they get is less and there is a, perhaps unspecified, hassle factor in the declaration and so on involved.

Neither danger need stop schemes being attractive, and some are set up in a way that provides payment to cover any additional tax due so that the net effect to the individual is positive. But such matters must be born in mind and details checked.

Note: the regulations on such matters are apt to change year by year, and they will certainly be different in different countries. The moral must be to check thoroughly so that nothing untoward is allowed to interfere with the positive effect of schemes you may embrace. The same applies to certain voucher and scratch card schemes, where some have run foul of legislation applicable to lotteries. As a general rule, if a scheme seems to good to be true, then it probably is.

maintaining interest

Even the best scheme will not last forever. Its appeal gradually fades, it is no longer new and exciting; nor does it motivate as much as it did when some time has passed. What is needed is a mix. For example:

- A package that includes elements that lend themselves to motivation.
- A basic underlying rewards scheme (such as commission or similar).
- A number of short-term schemes that are intentionally varied.

Change is then something that must be a permanent feature of the mix. Say people have a company car. The scheme will need regular review. Can the car be changed (perhaps introducing different grades)? Can choice be extended (perhaps adding to a list of choice factors that might include make, model, engine size, colour, body style, etc)? How about timing (perhaps with cars being changed more frequently)? And so on.

Such review is important. I can remember one company car scheme which for some reason (no doubt valid at the time, but lost in the mists of time) specified that only saloons could be chosen. This rule caused the motivational impact to be seriously diluted because the group of people in the scheme were predominantly at an age and stage where many had young families; they would mostly have favoured estate cars, and resented the seemingly nonsensical restriction.

The short-term schemes present a significant opportunity to ring the changes, to maintain interest and to involve everyone in the team. Instigate a new scheme and you can chart the interest graphically, as shown in Figure 6.1.

The new scheme generates rising interest, this is maintained for a while, and then gradually, or indeed less gradually, it declines. What works well therefore is a series of overlapping schemes: see Figure 6.2.

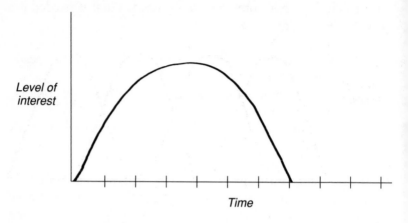

Figure 6.1 *Progress of interest generated by motivational scheme*

A series of schemes effectively maintains interest over the longer term. The four shown in Figure 6.2 might represent schemes that each ran for a quarter. The focus of each can be made a little different. In a customer care area, for example, one scheme might be concerned with recording the best customer response, another with keeping the level of complaints low, and so on. In this way you can prevent a focus that might allow the same person, or small group, to – as it were – win everything. The job of the schemes is to create and maintain excellent performance across the board. If schemes are constructed so that the same person inevitably comes top, others will quickly lose interest, the winner is seen as a fore-gone conclusion and everyone else works on as normal. Such may act to reward a high-flyer but will not fulfil the role of acting as an incentive to increase performance, lifting it above whatever it would have been without the scheme.

The other advantage of an overlapping series of schemes is that the whole cycle of introduction, explanation of new idea, working out of how it will work – and seeing if it will be fun –

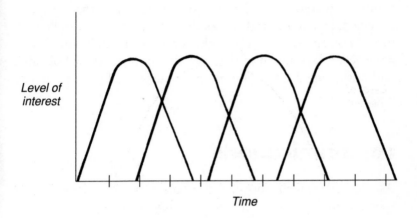

Figure 6.2 *Pattern of interest generated by overlapping schemes*

repeats. Some of the power of such a scheme comes not from the prospect of winning or making a gain, financial or otherwise; it works because the office is a social situation. People talk about it, they compare notes, possibly they compete and it adds to job interest – it creates a fun element in what may otherwise be a mundane day.

To act in this way needs more thought. You have got to come up with a series of interesting schemes, with differing focuses and prizes. But some will be natural developments of earlier ones, others will be suggested by the team and if they work then the time and effort is proved worthwhile. In some organizations and offices there are a considerable number of such things, some of which may be very simple and short term. For instance, something might be introduced at the start of a week – 'Whoever opens the most new accounts this week receives a (prize)' – to be replaced the next week by something else, perhaps more elaborate and lasting for a month. The only measure of how much of this sort of thing to do comes from the results. In some organizations and with some groups of people a plethora of fast-changing schemes is the norm, is expected, enjoyed... and works. For others such would be way too complicated. Take your pick, but do so carefully and, if you have never done much of this sort, do not reject the whole idea without giving it a try; you might be surprised by the results of a trial.

communications

As was mentioned above, the whole process of launching a scheme, of explaining it and charting its progress demands good communication. To maximize the effect:

- ■ This should be clear (people will not be motivated by what they do not understand).
- ■ Be accurate (put a decimal point in the wrong place so that people expect £1,000 instead of £100, and your scheme is doomed).
- ■ Keep it simple: make it seem easy to work out how the scheme is working and how an individual is doing so far at any point (if it is, or seems, too complex, people will not be bothered with it).
- ■ Engender some fun and excitement about it (so that people notice, take an interest and enjoy participating).
- ■ Link back to the business purpose (if the whole scheme is to increase productivity in some way, this should be clear).
- ■ Report the end result (if a scheme runs for a while and then just appears to disappear it negates its importance – a series of schemes should finish with a bang, and the finish of one should link to the start of another.

Remember it is not just the existence of a scheme that is important, nor its existing and working well – it is what is said about it that brings it to life. What you say about it starts the process, what the whole process encourages others to say adds to the impact.

extreme measures

Some things highlight the way motivation work, and while not making typical examples themselves give evidence that can prompt ideas that are right for you. Consider something like selling holiday timeshare. Not everyone's ideal occupation perhaps, and the presentations they use as a major part of their sales process are not everyone's cup of tea either.

Typically the people who work in this environment are paid on commission only. It may not be for you or your people, but it works for others. I have spoken to people working in such an environment and they love it (at least if they stay and succeed they do!). Yet there is uncertainty, high risk and many rejections. What is it that motivates? Is it the potential high rewards? To some extent yes, though the rewards may not in fact, even for those who succeed, be enormous compared with other occupations. More often it is the whole set-up: the rewards, the visibility of rewards, the targets (often repetitive and immediate, say daily) – and not least the competition between colleagues linked to the recognition of what individuals do, and perhaps also the feeling that this is not something at which just anyone could succeed.

The competitive element is a major one, and groups working this way often have a profusion of league tables and scoring systems designed to continually focus attention on the possibility of the next successful sale. One manager told me once that he had tangibly increased the power of such systems just by adding a photograph of each person to the already visibly displayed league table! Yet I see no reason to doubt he was right. The lesson here is not in trying to copy the complete system, but in noting how a scheme can be so well matched to the situation and to particular people and how a precise mix of activities then work together to achieve the desired effect.

A final point should be made about communications, showing the need to keep records, and the need not just for accuracy of communications, but careful checking to achieve it. An example demonstrates the dangers. For the first time Company A (who should, as you will see, remain anonymous) scheduled an annual conference overseas, also allowing staff to take their partners, and building in some free time. The event was very successful and after it motivation ran high. A year on, the manager responsible decided to repeat the idea; a new destination and venue were selected and, given the success of the social element, partners were again to be invited. In light of this the announcement, reminding of last year's event and setting out the details of the follow-up, was sent to people's homes. Replies quickly began to come in, together with several letters from the partners of various staff members saying: 'Just *what* conference was this last year?' It had been someone else who had accompanied the employee to the previous event. Oops! On that note illustrating the need for care in communications, we will turn to broader issues about the potential motivational power of communications which deserves its own chapter.

the contribution of communication

Motivation is nothing if not multifaceted, and every single element of it is bound up with communication, as is the whole process of management itself for that matter – no communication, no management.

The implications here are clear. Not only is motivation itself primarily executed through communication, but the precise form of that communication needs to be born in mind and contributes directly to the effect achieved.

Perhaps the first thing to recognize is that sometimes the opportunity to motivate and do so successfully is dependent mostly on the *way things are communicated*. The following case, something I was involved in a while ago, reinforces this point.

Example: communications – big problem, small problem
A travel agent is essentially a service and people business. In one particular firm, with a chain of some 30 retail outlets across several counties, business was lagging behind targets. The industry was, at the time, not in recession. Rather the lag was due to competitive activity, and was something that a more active,

sales-oriented approach could potentially cure. Initially the managers' approach to the problem was to draw attention to the problem at every level. Memos were circulated to all staff. The figures – the sales revenue planned for the business, the amount coming from holidays, flights, etc – were substantial figures; even the shortfall was some hundreds of thousands of pounds.

The result? Well, certainly the sales graph did not rise. But, equally certainly, morale dropped. People went from feeling they worked for a successful organization to thinking it was – at worst – foundering; and feeling that the fault was being laid at their door. The figures meant little to the kind of young people who manned the counters – they were just unimaginably large numbers to which they were wholly unable to relate personally.

With a sales conference coming, a different strategy was planned. The large shortfall was amortized and presented as a series of smaller figures – one per branch. These 'catch-up' figures were linked to what needed to be sold, in addition to normal business, in order to catch up and hit target. It amounted, if I remember right, to two additional holidays (mum, dad and 2.2 children) per branch, per week. Not only was this something staff could easily relate to, it was something they understood and felt they could actually achieve. Individual targets, ongoing communication to report progress and some prizes for branches hitting and bettering these targets in a number of ways completed the picture.

The result this time? The numbers slowly climbed. The gap closed. Motivation increased with success in sight. A difficult year ended with the company hitting the original planned targets – and motivation returned, continuing to run high as a real feeling of achievement was felt.

The key factor here was, I am sure, one of communications. The numbers and the difficulty of hitting them did not change. The perception of the problem, however, was made manageable, personal and – above all – was made to seem achievable. The results then showed that success was possible. No significant costs were involved here, just a little thought and time to make sure the communications were right, that motivation was positively affected and that results stood a real chance of rising.

In many such circumstances, a positive impact is made more likely on many problems if motivation is used to influence people. As a last thought about this example, it should be said that while the difficulties that were surmounted by the travel company make it a good example, the same principles apply to *positive* situations. It is as important, and often easier, to build on success as to tackle difficulties, indeed this may produce the greatest return for the action taken. But this is only the case if the communication with people is clear, and messages are put in a way that makes them easy to relate to.

Communication is something influenced by many things: who is being communicated with, the circumstances, the method being used, the intention behind it and, of course, who is doing it. Think of a very simple message. When Clint Eastwood (playing a tough and uncompromising cop in the Dirty Harry movies) says 'Make my day', it carries enough power not only to make the villain cringe, but to move the phrase into the language. Why? Because the way it was said was influenced by all the things just mentioned. The same phrase said in a different way, by someone in different circumstances could equally mean nothing and be instantly forgotten. Similarly, how your communications goes over, and more particularly whether it acts to motivate or not, is dependent on a number of things.

All the factors, whether positive or negative and stemming from the intrinsic qualities of human nature, contribute to the process that can used by management and can play their part in ensuring that people want to perform and perform well. Communication is a vital part of this picture. Every piece of communication, and there are many, can have motivational overtones – and probably will. For example, put in a new system, say asking people to fill in a new form on a regular basis, and – if it is not made clear why it is useful – people will be demotivated. This is because it relates to the list of dissatisfiers – specifically policy and administration – and they will probably just see it as a time-consuming chore. Similarly, a wealth of communications affect the motivational climate, jogging the overall measure of it one way or the other, for example:

- ■ *job descriptions, clear guidelines and adequate training:* all give a feeling of security, without which motivation suffers;
- ■ *incentives:* will work less effectively if their details are not clearly communicated (for instance, an incentive payment scheme may be allowed to seem so complicated that no one works out how they are doing and motivation suffers as a result);
- ■ *routine jobs:* can be made more palatable by communicating to people what an important contribution they make;
- ■ *job titles:* may sensibly be chosen with an eye on how they affect people's feelings of status as well as acting as a description of function ('Sales Executive' may be fine and clear to customers, but most prefer titles like 'Account Service Manager' which seem to bestow more status).

Every aspect of communications may itself be affected by a whole list of different factors relating to the circumstances, the people, and, of course, their instigator. Management style – you and how you operate – is key among such factors, and worth a few words.

the contribution of management style

The kind of manager you are will certainly affect the ease with which you can motivate people; and thus the time and effort involved. Perhaps the first principle any manager should adopt is to be, and remain, well informed about the prevailing motivational status of any group for whom he or she is responsible.

There is more to this than simply asking. Indeed, just saying 'Anything worrying you?' to people, especially when there is something (and perhaps they feel you should know), is not always likely to get a straight answer. People may want to tell you that you are getting right up their nose in some way, but bite their tongue, or they may not mention things they feel you would see as trivial. You need to be more subtle in investigation. Read between the lines, observe people's behaviour and how they react to things. Use the grapevine, gleaning informal comment to put alongside – and weigh carefully with – harder evidence.

Constant vigilance is useful, both to avoid missing opportunities to add positively to the situation, and to avoid unrest creeping up on you and only presenting itself when it has become a significant problem. The formalities of this were explored earlier.

Managers must manage. It is a process that demands some personal clout. But there is, in fact, an overlap between the characteristics that staff approve of and look for in their 'ideal' manager, and those necessary to being an effective manager. A good manager is fair, approachable, decisive, respects his or her staff and their point of view, and is honest (and not unnecessarily secretive). Good communication is also very important. So too is that people feel they benefit positively from the relationship – indeed highest of all among desired characteristics people often put 'working for someone I learn from'.

Also high on the list, people value consistency. If you run hot and cold, are sweetness and light one minute and doom, gloom and overbearing the next, people will understandably find you difficult to relate to. It helps too if managers are seen as being good at their own job. And, despite the old saying that you do not have to be able to lay eggs to be a chicken farmer, it helps if you at least understand the details of the tasks others have to work on.

Note too that the most motivational style aims high. People like to work in an environment of success in which challenges are set, people pull together and everyone sees the results of their efforts. They do not like 'passengers' being tolerated, and this too has implications for managing people.

If some of these characteristics are not your natural character, then you may need actively to inject a bit more of them into your style. Think of what you would want from your own manager; and remember that it works both ways. The remainder of this chapter looks at particular elements of management style that are disproportionately important in their motivational effect.

the role of communication

Being on the receiving end of good, clear communications is certainly motivational. Organizations characterized by people never really knowing what is going on, not being clear about objectives, policy or instructions, rarely show evidence of high morale.

Because communication is inherently difficult (when was the last occasion on which you spent unnecessary time sorting out the results of some communication breakdown?), it needs thought and care. The detail of:

- ■ choice of communications method (eg memo, meeting, e-mail, etc),
- ■ clarity of message (eg sufficient background),
- ■ building in opportunity for feedback (or not),
- ■ timing (eg ahead of any rumours),
- ■ who is communicated with (and who is not)

are, like all such factors, important to the way the communication is received and judged. Thus to seek comment from staff, but condition the request – 'I think this is a good idea, what do you think?' (with the subtext seeming to be: disagree if you dare), is certainly not motivational. Meetings make another good example and involve a great panoply of communications situations. Do *you* like sitting in a meeting that starts late and is rushed, disorganized and run without firm chairmanship so that no one feels able to put their point or thinks that it will be listened to if they do? No. And nor do the people who attend your meetings.

If you are a good communicator, if you write and present well, know the rules of chairing a meeting and bring care and concern for the motivational implications of your every communication, you will find the advantages to your staff are appreciated. If you can identify any weaknesses among this kind of skill, for example the ability to effectively chair a meeting, then these may need addressing. Only if you can perform such tasks well will it be possible to motivate through them.

Finally, informal communication is as important as formal. A good manager does not just keep people informed through discussion and sending memos (indeed, too many of those can be demotivational), they make the workplace fun. This is not overstating the point. Business is a serious business, but this should not make it dull. Most people spend more time at work than in any other way; they want it to be fun, and managers who recognize this will motivate better than those who do not. Certain specifics of communication are now reviewed by taking a number of examples of what must be done.

consultation

This is more than simply communicating. That can be one-way, whereas consultation is essentially two-way, with listening to, collecting, considering and ultimately building in other people's views being inherent to the process. People like to be consulted. They believe their opinions matter and that their ideas might be useful. And they are right. So adopting a consultative approach to management boosts motivation, but this is not the only reason for it – it helps with what you are trying to achieve as well.

Of course, there are some things about which there is no merit in engaging in elaborate consultation. Being selective allows time for others where it is worthwhile – you must select what goes in which camp. Not consulting on some things can thus be motivational, provided that people understand that this is done to give consultation time to other, more important, topics. Having said that, consulting can be very useful. Two heads really are often better than one; well conceived and executed, consultation around a team works.

You may usefully build in, or increase, consultation in regular processes – the departmental meetings you already hold perhaps – or convene formal sessions just for this process. A useful part of it is essentially informal: stopping someone on the stairs just to ask 'What do you think about... ?' All types of consultation have their place and will be appreciated.

There is one danger here: the kind of manager who consults and then passes others' ideas on around the organization as if they were their own is deeply resented. Do not try to get all the credit. Being generous with the credit, for example labelling something as a subordinate's idea even when you made a major contribution or cajoled them into the thinking that produced it, is powerful motivation. After all, you get the credit for creating and maintaining a first-class team. If you want to make things happen, use the giving of credit to boost idea generation and motivation in parallel. It provides a powerful combination.

development

Top of the list of almost any survey I have ever seen asking: 'What makes a good manager?' is, as was mentioned earlier, a comment about him or her being someone people want to work for: 'someone I learn from'. No one wants to stand still, and we all know the thought, mentioned earlier, that there is an important difference between five years' experience and one year's experience repeated five times. Which would you choose?

Development – training in all its forms – is motivational. Again this is something with a dual purpose. Developing people's skills is useful to the organization as well as to individuals; it can positively boost results and motivation together. From the management point of view it perhaps makes good sense to divide the methodology into two: individual mentoring and group development.

mentoring

A mentor is someone who spends time, individually and often informally, with people to help them accelerate their experience and improve their competencies. Mentoring takes some time, but the results and resultant good motivation can be very worthwhile.

You need to relate this activity to some sort of overall development plan, and ensure that the whole process grows in effectiveness through the momentum and continuity of the process. Your staff will get used to these informal sessions and, finding them useful, will work at getting more from them. Just a 10-minute digression during a meeting convened to progress some project may be necessary. Alternatively, you may be able to think of ways to incorporate advice and assistance into normal ongoing business processes. For example, to include an element of development activity on an important topic, some managers create a formality about certain internal meetings, making staff deliver their points as formal 'on your feet' presentations. This is an important skill, one helped by practice – doing this and adding a few words of critique or encouragement adds only a few moments to the meeting and is useful for all concerned.

planned development activity

Here the range of options is vast. People can attend courses (arranged 'in-company' or as 'public' events), but a host of lesser things are useful also. You can recommend that staff read a business book, go to a showing of a training film (some companies have in-house showings at lunchtime), attend a conference, trade fair or other event, or work through some programmed training material (say on CD-ROM).

All such activity can be made motivational, provided it is relevant and useful. Introducing new skills, some with an eye on the future rather than immediate needs, updating or upgrading others, correcting weaknesses and building on strengths – all can be part of your overall motivation.

Remember training and development do not have to appear as such, it is often more useful for someone to be involved in a project from which they will learn something – so the motivational effect of development can pervade many management processes. Here mentoring and development overlap. A final point here about development is worth comment.

training evaluation

Most organizations have some level of ongoing training and development activity. Some of this is formal: attending a course. This is a good example of an activity where simple documentation linked to the event can have a motivational role and assist measurement. Most staff who are asked to complete a post-course evaluation form will do so, and will see being asked to as itself motivational ('They care about whether this was useful or not').

Even a simple form – see the example in Figure 7.1 – can act to measure the effectiveness of training, while also casting some light on the motivation of people completing them. Such a form does not have to remain the same for ever. Some companies change such devices regularly, in part to include additional – maybe topical – questions that are useful at the time.

delegation

Who do you want to work for: someone who is a good delegator or someone who is not? No contest; and those who work for you feel the same. If you are busy, and most managers are, then delegation can help you fit more in as well as allowing you to concentrate on key issues. It also ensures that things are regularly exposed to new thinking and new approaches; this is in major part how organizations change, grow and improve. Do you really believe you have a monopoly on common sense, and that no one can do things as well as you can? More often fear of someone doing something better than us is a prime reason why delegation does *not* happen as much as it should (be honest!). Of course, delegation needs to be carried out effectively:

- selecting appropriate tasks;
- selecting the right people;
- giving clear, well-communicated briefings;
- building in agreed, planned checks, if necessary;
- not watching every move;
- evaluating the results afterwards.

When it works well, delegation helps you by freeing up time that can be spent on key tasks. It helps staff by giving them new challenges, new tasks to handle as part of their work portfolio, and acting to help develop or improve new skills and evolve new approaches in the process.

the Institute of Management

COURSE ASSESSMENT

OPEN PROGRAMMES

Please complete this form before you leave, as this will help our future planning. As we are also interested in the long-term value of our training programmes we shall contact a sample of participants by telephone after the course to ask for their comments. I would like to thank you in advance for your help.

Pippa Bourne

Course Title.. Date................................

Name .... Job Title ....

Organisation ....

Training Manager's Name .... Telephone number ....

Please circle the appropriate response.	Comment *(Please comment on your response rating)*
1. What is your overall opinion of the course? 1 2 3 4 5 6 very good very poor	
2. How would you rate the Course Leader's presentation? 1 2 3 4 5 6 very good very poor	
3. In your opinion, did the course meet the objectives set out in the course brochure? 1 2 3 4 5 6 very well very poorly	
4. What is your opinion of the course materials? *(Course papers, visual aids etc)* 1 2 3 4 5 6 very good very poor	
5. What was your opinion of the venue? 1 2 3 4 5 6 very good very poor	
6. How well was your booking/enquiry dealt with? 1 2 3 4 5 6 very well very poorly	

7. Was the level of content? *(Please tick appropriate box)*	
Much too advanced ☐ Too advanced ☐ Just right ☐ Too basic ☐ Much too basic ☐	
8. Do you feel the course can be improved by the inclusion or expansion of certain topics? *(If so, which?)*	
9. In your opinion would the course work better without certain topics? *(If so, which?)*	
10. Has the course provided you with any ideas or actions which could be implemented at work?	
11. Was sufficient time allowed to answer your questions and discuss your particular issues?	Yes ☐ No ☐
12. Would you recommend the course to a colleague?	Yes ☐ No ☐
13. If the answer to the above question was 'no', why not?	
14. Was it your idea to attend the course?	Yes ☐ No ☐
15. If not, who brought it to your attention (name and job title please)?	
16. Were you given a copy of our short course brochure to see the course content?	Yes ☐ No ☐
17. What other course subjects are of interest to you?	

18. How did your organisation hear about the course?		
IM Brochure	*(Please state how obtained)*	....
Advertisement	*(Please state which)*	....
Within own organisation	*(Please give details)*	....
Other source	*(Please give details)*	....

☐ If you are interested in running this course tailored to your organisation's requirements, please tick this box and we will contact you.

Figure 7.1 *Training course evaluation form*

Note: Thanks are due to the Institute of Management for permission to reproduce this form, one used as an integral part of their short course programme.

The motivational effect of such monitoring can be enhanced by the routine of inviting people to sit down with you after they have undertaken training to discuss what was learnt and review action for the future. Giving time to this bestows an importance on it and also provides a real chance that useful action will be put in train for the future; and that is the ultimate motivator.

appraisal

Let us be honest. Not every appraisal meeting held in every organization is constructive and useful. Too often they are regarded as academic (in the worst sense of the word), as a waste of time (and yet often also as worrying) by both those who run appraisal meetings and those who attend them. Yet, well conducted, they represent a major opportunity.

How can a job be satisfying if the incumbent has no idea whether what they are doing is well regarded or not? The principle of achievement and recognition of achievement has already been touched on. It is a powerful motivator.

Appraisals, both the once- or twice-a-year formal sessions that are typical in many organizations and the ongoing informal discussions that may sensibly be included as part of the process, can be so useful. They act to:

■ review the past year;
■ plan the next year;
■ formalize training and development plans;
■ spark ideas;
■ relate to long-term career development.

They are often, though not necessarily rightly, linked to review of salary and other rewards (*note*: there is a strong case for separating the two things to allow the appraisal meeting to concentrate on the review of practice and change for the future).

The better the appraisal system, and the more constructively you run appraisal meetings for those for whom you are responsible the more you will get from the process in terms of positive motivation. The key rules are to:

■ ensure the system used is logical, sound and focused on change for the future;

- plan how you will conduct meetings in advance;
- give due notice and briefing to those being appraised to allow them time to prepare;
- ensure the majority of the time is allowed for the person being appraised to talk (it is not simply an opportunity for you to tell them things);
- focus discussion primarily on the future rather than the past.

Reviewing the past is only useful as a way to make future operations more certain – viewed this way appraisals can be constructive, useful and motivational. Appraisals make an excellent example of the kind of management process that acts – or can do so – as a significant motivation and is itself important enough to review in more detail. Few activities within an organization are both so important and yet have a tendency to be so inadequately carried out. Appraisals are not only important to the process of managing people, they are important to the achievement of their future objectives. They act in part to look back, and more importantly to look ahead. When they are well conducted, they are both practically useful, helping to ensure the achievement of the performance that is required in future, and are also themselves part of the motivational process. In other words staff should find their appraisals motivational, interesting and constructive; and that they provide useful feedback and act as a catalyst to future action.

The first task in considering appraisals is to be sure that the content of the appraisal is well specified. There are dangers in measuring, or trying to, attributes that are inherent to personality. There are also specific areas where measurement and rating is not the appropriate way of dealing with them. To take an extreme example, in most organizations people are either rated as honest or fired. Yet one still occasionally sees such factors as 'honesty' listed as headings to be rated out of 10 on company appraisal systems.

The prevailing approach to appraisal these days majors on

competencies. These can start with common factors, but the relevance of each must be fitted to every individual group of staff. Table 7.1 gives an indication of the sort of factors many organizations will use as a starting point for the design of appraisal systems, and of the details inherent within the main points. These sorts of areas normally go hand in hand with a review of the achievement of specific results for which an individual is responsible (and on which they may have specific targets).

Table 7.1 *Competencies that can act as the basis of appraisal*

Achievement of objectives: any targets and results areas that are relevant.

- *Leadership:* directing and motivating others towards clear objectives.
- *Management:* day-to-day supervision of team-working, delegation, and all the other management skills (including appraisal).
- *Relationships:* up, down and around the organization.
- *Strategy:* overall vision, looking to the long term, general commercial awareness.
- *Drive:* self-motivation, persistence, energy and enthusiasm put into things.
- *Communication:* effectiveness of all forms of communication (written, oral or in particular forms, eg presentations), listening.
- *Working manner:* adaptability and flexibility, time management.
- *Analysis:* problem solving, numeracy, data collection and handling.
- *Implementation:* making decisions, planning, organizing and getting things done.
- *Creativity:* idea generation, open-mindedness.
- *Personal:* concerns for the organization and others, integrity, career focus.

Note: any such headings must be interpreted in light of the nature of an individual organization and its staff. Additional headings may need to be added, and individual headings may need a clear list of subheadings that go into some detail. For example, the heading 'Analysis' above might need spelling out, listing such factors as: a measure of analytical skills and the ability to collect, organize, work with and present numerical (and financial) data in order to support or document particular projects. The nature of the projects an individual worked on might allow further personalization of such a list.

As an appraisal meeting follows its chosen agenda, and reviews various factors concerned in employee's performance, it should present no problem to incorporate the opportunity to obtain feedback regarding how somebody feels about the job they are doing and the circumstances in which they are required to do it. But this will only work if the appraisal meeting itself is well conducted and the appraisee sees it as being constructive – for them as well as for the organization. Its being well conducted will depend on appropriate preparation and the meeting itself being conducted in the right kind of way. The checklist in Table 7.2 highlights the key issues of both stages.

Table 7.2 *Checklist for appraisal conduct*

---

1. Preparation
    ■ Prepare written notification that explains the nature of the meeting and specifies any necessary preparation on the part of the appraisee as well as setting time and place.
    ■ Study the job holder's records and collect any other factual information about performance that is necessary.
    ■ Check that any standards by which performance is measured remain appropriate.
    ■ Make notes setting out your views about the appraisee on the evidence to date (though do not try to make any overall rating ahead of the meeting).

Table 7.2 *(cont'd)*

- Check that you can justify any opinions (asking yourself why you think something).
- Consider and note any development needs for the future.
- Set down any ideas for future projects or involvements for the appraisee.
- Consult with any other people who may know or supervise the appraisee to fill out the picture you are forming.
- Anticipate questions that may be raised at the meeting and make sure you have both what and why answers ready.

2. The interview
   - Allow enough time.
   - Arrange that the meeting is uninterrupted.
   - Choose a comfortable environment.
   - Put the appraisee at their ease early on.
   - Spell out the purpose of the meeting clearly before getting into particulars.
   - Direct the conversation (with your agenda in mind).
   - Concentrate on the implications for the future.
   - Listen (the appraisee should do most of the talking).
   - Prevent digressions (eg salary may be dealt with separately and need avoiding at this stage).
   - Concentrate on performance factors (rather than amateur attempts to measure personality).
   - Use the appraisal form (there should be one), working through the logical review it should set out and doing so in sequence.
   - Encourage discussion of both strengths and weaknesses (and areas for improvement).
   - Make any ratings element clear at the end of the meeting.
   - Double-check any action points that are agreed to take place (who will do what, and when).
   - End with a thank you.

A well-conducted appraisal meeting will give some indication of an individual's current motivation. In addition the appraiser should have specific topics within the meeting planned as areas of motivational investigation. For example: discussion of communication between people (whether with colleagues or manager to subordinate) can be used to cast light on the working arrangement and how someone feels about it; and discussion about particular tasks might allow feelings about how people, organization or equipment assisted or hindered the effective performance of the task.

If there are particular known areas for investigation then the agenda, preparation and time allowed should all facilitate this aspect of the process. Although motivational investigation must not be allowed to take over the main purpose of the meeting, such a formal session can cast considerable light on a person's motivational state. Clearly the more constructive the feeling towards appraisal is, the more likely it is that honest – and constructive – comments will be made about matters that affect motivation. Another, though less regular, kind of meeting might be regarded as an appraisal of a different kind: meetings run at the end of someone's period of employment.

exit interviews

The term 'exit interviews' is used to describe a meeting with someone about to leave the organization to move to another employer (or for any other reason: they might be retiring or be starting to work freelance). These meetings can be held for various reasons; for example, they will sometimes be held to try to persuade someone to stay rather than leave. Here the term is used in the sense of fact-finding meetings designed to obtain information from someone when the decision to leave is firm. The purpose is to look ahead, and is specifically concerned with assisting the maintenance, retention and motivation of *other* staff in future. Information so obtained can help make either the attractions of our organization greater, or those of others less so by comparison.

One caveat should be mentioned before making any further comment about exit interviews. That is the question of who is responsible for conducting them. As it is clearly vital to create a situation where people are motivated to provide honest and open information, it may be better that such interviews are *not* conducted by the immediate line manager of whoever is leaving (they could just be one of the reasons for their departure!). In a large organization this may make the Personnel section the natural choice; an alternative and one that works well when there is no formal Personnel function is a swap arrangement – a line manager in one section will conduct exit interviews for staff from another section and vice versa.

There are two distinct areas of information that are worth preparing for (just like appraisals, exit interviews need to be well set up, to have a clear agenda and to be conducted in the right environment). These are: *reasons for leaving* and *experience while in the job*. The first is an important element of external intelligence. It can provide information on a number of factors such as how salary and benefits compare with the market and with specific competitors, or with working environments on offer elsewhere. Such information may lead directly to further checking and comparison and thus to action that is beneficial to staffing situations in the future.

The second should address both positive and negative factors. Most people do not leave because they have come to dislike *everything* about an organization. The longer they have worked there, the more useful it may be to hear what has kept them there. But certain dissatisfactions may be inherent in their decision to leave. Some may come from factors that are unavoidable and do not need prompt action. Other negative feelings may be a sign of dangers that need sorting out for the future. If most people moving on from a particular department consistently complain that the style in which they were managed was oppressive, then this may indicate that further investigation is advisable.

Exit interviews are a good example of techniques that work best if they are part of the culture of the organization, ie if it is understood that they happen, that they are practical and that they serve a constructive purpose, then those who attend them are more likely to co-operate with them. Not least they provide a formal opportunity to say a thank you for past services and ensure that people leave on good terms (you never know when and in what circumstances you may meet them again). If the kinds of opportunity evidenced here are sought out, and then set up and implemented carefully, they can play a significant part in the ongoing process of monitoring prevailing motivational levels.

communication

Some of the foregoing, like job appraisal meetings, are very specific communications, but the range of things to be done varies enormously – from just a word or two to a complex ongoing campaign of communications involving numbers of discussions, meetings and exchanges. Communication constitutes so much of the management job that it is especially important to develop habits here. In a busy moment (and in less busy ones) it is all too easy to snap out an order, dismiss the need for consultation or ignore something without thinking about the motivational implications of what you are doing.

example: a powerful phrase

One commonly experienced situation provides a useful example here. Imagine: you are sitting in your office when a head comes round the door, and someone asks you for your help. Busy, you quickly ask what the problem is and, in order to get them on their way and you back to your task, you offer a brief, instant solution – 'do so and so'. They depart.

They can get on. So can you. But are they any happier for the experience? Probably not. What is the alternative? Well, it takes a little longer, though not in the long term. Imagine the same request for advice. This time you act to make them think and will say only 'What do you think you should do?' Either then or later (you can get them to come back in a few minutes) they must offer an opinion. This may be something you can approve – 'Good idea, seems fine to me' – or it may be something you can get them to work on – 'I'm sure that's in the right direction, how would it work in practice?' Ask questions to prompt discussion and get them to arrive at an acceptable way forward.

In the latter case, several things happen:

- they learn something;
- their confidence increases;
- they are less likely to come in so often with similar queries (because they know you will not provide an easy solution);
- you spend a little more time up front, but save some in the longer term.

So it is a useful response – it motivates, aids development (which motivates), helps create a constructive relationship between manager and managed (which motivates), saves time (certainly for the manager)... and gets the right thing done. Perhaps it also boosts responsibility and increases self-sufficiency, making it more likely that the right action will be taken next time you are not there to ask and something *must* be done. Two aspects occur repeatedly throughout all the thinking here: the need to ask, and the need to listen. It is all too easy to plough on with your own work, hoping other people will do the same. You really cannot ask staff too many questions, it acts to:

- involve them, and make them feel important;
- ensure accuracy of action (and avoid fire-fighting and reinventing the wheel);

- keep you informed;
- secure specific information;
- prompt idea generation;
- smooth the implementation of change;
- give *you* better management control, as a more self-sufficient team allows you to concentrate on key issues.

If questions are important, and you could surely add to the above list and make it more specific, then listening to the answers is important too (see page 65). This is not only so that you hear, and can thus act on, what is said, it is also so that you are *seen* to be taking an interest – so that people feel that what they have to say matters and makes a difference. It does and it should. You would surely not want to have a team capable only of doing the bare minimum and contributing nothing to the broader picture.

Nothing is more likely to demotivate people than them feeling that their manager does not care what they think, especially when they are convinced (often correctly) that what they think can contribute and help. No manager can get so close to the detail that what others who are actually involved in that detail think does not matter. At the end of the day, communication pervades the entire motivational process. Its importance must not be underestimated, thus we shall return to some of the factors just reviewed in the remaining text.

involvement and empowerment

Management fads seem to follow each other much as do the seasons, sometimes lasting no longer. The word 'empowerment' enjoyed a brief vogue in the late 1990s and, if you believe the hype, it was yet another concept guaranteed to solve all problems and put any organization securely on the road to success. If only. On the other hand, there is considerable sense in the idea of empowerment. It may not solve everything, but it is useful and it does provide additional bite to the prevailing motivational feeling.

putting empowerment to work

Rather than describe leaden definitions, let us start with an example. The Ritz-Carlton group has enjoyed good publicity not only for the undoubted quality of its many hotels, but for a particular policy it operates. Say you are staying in one of its hotels and have (perish the thought) something to complain about. So, reeling from the stench from your minibar or whatever, you stick your head out of your bedroom door into the corridor and take up the matter with a passing chambermaid.

Now whoever you were to speak to the procedure would be the same. *Every* single member of the hotel's staff is briefed to be able to handle your complaint. They do not have to find a supervisor, check with the manager or thumb through the rule-book. They fix it, as they think fit. And they have a prearranged budget to back up their chosen action – every single member of staff can spend so many dollars (I think it started as US $500, but it has no doubt changed) instantly, and without any checks, to satisfy a guest's complaint.

So, to continue our example, if the minibar was dirty they could summon someone to clean it at once (even if that meant paying overtime). They could refill it with complimentary drinks and throw in a free bottle of fine wine and a bowl of fruit on a side table to make up to the guest for the inconvenience. Such staff are empowered.

It is an approach that gets things done. It regards staff as a key resource, not only one to get tasks completed but one that can, in many ways, decide just how best they can get it done. The empowerment approach goes way beyond simple delegation and plays on the appeal of responsibility to the individual to get things done and done right. It works in part because staff like it – because being empowered, being given responsibility in such an overt way, is motivational.

making empowerment possible

On the other hand, empowerment does not allow managers to abrogate their responsibility, nor does it represent anarchy, a free-for-all where anything goes. The chambermaid (mentioned above) does not have the right to do just anything, only to select, or invent, something that will meet the customer's needs and which does not cost more than the budget to implement.

Staying with our hotel example, consider what must lie in the background. Staff must:

- ■ *understand guests*, their expectations and their likely reaction to difficulties (and how that might be compounded by circumstances – having to check out quickly to catch a flight, for example);
- ■ *be proficient at handling complaints*, communicating skilfully so as to deal with anything that might occur promptly, politely and efficiently;
- ■ *have in mind typical solutions* and be able to improvise to produce better or more appropriate solutions to match the customer situation;
- ■ *know the system:* what cost limit exists, what documentation needs completing afterwards, who needs to be communicated with, etc.

The systems – rules – aspect is, however, minimal. There is no need for forms to be filled in in advance, no hierarchy of supervisors who have to be consulted – most of what must happen is left to the discretion of the individual members of staff (though if the need arises management can be involved). The essence of such empowerment is a combination of self-sufficiency based on a solid foundation of training and management practices that ensure that staff will be able to do the right thing.

letting go

Often, when I conduct training courses, the room is full of managers tied as if by umbilical cord to their mobile telephones or pagers. Many of the calls that are made in the breaks are not responses to messages, they are made just to 'see everything is all right'. Are such calls, or the vast majority of them, really necessary? I wonder.

The opposite of this situation is more instructive. See if this rings a bell. You get back to the office after a gap (a business trip, holiday, whatever). Everything seems to be in order. When you examine some of the things that have been actioned in your absence you find that your view is that staff have made exactly the right decisions, yet... you know that *if you had been in the office, they would have asked you about some of the issues involved.* Some of the time staff empower themselves, and when they do, what they do is very often right.

All empowerment does is put this kind of process on a formal footing. It promotes the concept of ownership. It creates more self-reliant staff, able to consider what to do, make appropriate decisions and execute the necessary action successfully. Perhaps we should all allow this to happen more often and more easily.

making empowerment effective

Empowerment cannot be seen as an isolated process. It is difficult to view it other than as an integral part of the overall management process. You can only set out to create a feeling of empowerment by utilizing a range of other specific management processes to that end, though the process perhaps starts with attitude and communication. What degree of autonomy do your staff feel you allow them? If they feel restricted and, at worst, under control every moment of the day, they will tend to perform less well. Allowing such feeling is certainly a good way to stifle initiative and creativity.

So you need to let it be known that you expect a high degree of self-sufficiency, define what that means and manage in a way that makes it possible. All sorts of things contribute, but the following are key:

■ *Clear policy:* empowerment will only ever work if everyone understands the intentions of the organization (or department) and their role (clear job descriptions), so as to allow them to put any action they may need to decide upon in context. Another requirement of an empowered group is an absence of detailed rules to be followed slavishly. Rather, what is needed is the provision of clear guidelines about the results to be aimed at and the methods to be deployed (with these, better still, being worked out in consultation in a way that involves people and makes what is decided 'our' guidelines).

■ *Good communication:* this has been mentioned before in the context of motivation, indeed it has its own chapter. Any organization can easily be stifled by lack of, or lack of clarity in, communication; an empowered group is doubly affected by this failing.

■ *Little interference:* management must set things up so that people can be self-sufficient, and then keep largely clear. Developing the habit of taking the initiative is quickly stifled if staff know nothing they do will be able to be completed without endless checks (mostly, they will feel, made just at the wrong moment). If management is constantly taking over or taking all the credit, then interference will become a prime moan.

■ *Consultation:* a management style in which consultation is inherent acts as the best foundation for an empowered way of operating. It means that the framework within which people take responsibility is not simply wished, perhaps seemingly unthinkingly, upon them, but is something they helped define – and of which they have taken ownership.

■ *Feedback:* empowerment needs to maintain itself, actions taken must not sink into a rut and cease to be appropriate because time has passed and no one has considered the implications of change. Feedback may only be a manifestation of consultation, but some controls are also necessary. Certainly the overall ethos must be one of dynamism, continuing to search for better and better ways to do things as a response to external changes in a dynamic, and competitive, world.

■ *Development:* it is axiomatic that if people are to be empowered, they must be competent to execute the tasks required of them and to do so well. This ties in with what has already been said about training and development.

An enlightened attitude to development is motivational. A well-trained team of people is better able to be empowered, it has the confidence and the skills. An empowered and competent team is more likely to produce better productivity and performance. It is a virtuous circle.

towards excellence

At the end of the day the answer is in your hands. Keep too tight a reign on people and they will no doubt perform, but they may lack the enthusiasm to excel. Management should have nothing less than excellence of performance as its aim – market pressures mean any other view risks the organization being vulnerable to events and competitive action. On the other hand, too little control, an abrogation of responsibility and control, also creates risk, in this case that staff will fly off at a tangent, losing sight of their objectives and, at worst, doing no more than what takes their fancy.

Like so much else a balance is necessary. Empowerment is not a panacea, but an element of this philosophy can enhance the performance of most teams. Achievement and responsibility ranked high in the review of positive motivators in Chapter 4. Empowerment embodies both. Motivation will always remain a matter of detail, with management seeking to obtain the most powerful cumulative impact from the sum total of their actions, while keeping the time and cost of so doing within sensible bounds.

Empowerment is one more arrow in the armoury of potential techniques available to you, but it is an important one. Incorporate it in what becomes the right mix of ideas and methods for you, your organization and your people, and it can help make the whole work effectively.

action plan

At the end of the day managers must not only understand motivation in a general sense, they must approach it actively and systematically to create influences that constantly test, modify and enhance the prevailing motivational climate. They must also look ahead, and anticipate any factors that may influence things, so that they can plan responses in advance rather than as a response to the actual event.

Any action must be precise, well chosen and implemented, and right for the people on the receiving end, as it were. Before looking at how to be sure action does occur, we will examine making it appropriate on an individual basis.

linking to specific staff

The principles of motivation are a practical guide, but every employee is an individual and any tendency to think that everyone will respond to the same things in the same way must be resisted. The nature of the people, and of the job they do, both have a bearing on their situation. To have any effect, action to change and improve motivation must be well targeted, and that means taking understanding to a very specific level.

Some general issues will be important to most categories of staff. But not all the specific factors mentioned are valid for everyone. Similarly, there will be additional factors that may be important in a specific context. For example:

- not everyone has a company car, or even an office;
- only certain employees travel;
- some jobs are inherently more interesting than others;
- some people work in teams, others more individually;
- some supervise others, others are themselves supervised, etc.

Table 9.1 shows examples of the kind of question that needs to be asked in order to prepare a list of factors reflecting the position of individual employees or employee groups. Always be careful *never* to be censorious and add to, or remove, items from the list on the basis of your own motivations; there is no reason why you should view matters the same way as others do. And any kind of difference between yourself and members of your team – age, experience, background, or responsibilities – may make it likely that such different perceptions are the norm.

While the headings in Table 9.1 will always provide a good starting point (and some of the questions shown as general examples may also be useful pointers), such a checklist must be personalized specifically to an individual organization and often also to different categories of staff. For instance, for customer-contact staff working on the telephone at a computer terminal, questions about working conditions can focus on the systems and equipment they use and how they facilitate the level of service they are able to give customers as well as, say, their productivity. Once you are clear about the precise links between action and people you can proceed to actually take action.

Table 9.1 *Personalizing motivational action*

Company policy and administration	Supervision	Interpersonal	Working relationship	Personal life conditions	Security	Status	Salary
What systems do staff use?	Do manager/subordinate styles match?	Do people work in teams?	Are conditions seen as attractive?	Are hours of work regarded as sensible?	Does everyone have a job description?	Do people feel valued?	Are salaries seen as fair internally?
What forms must they fill in, how often and how many?	Is communication adequate and constructive?	Are there inappropriate cliques in the section?	Is equipment regarded as suitable?	Is the duration of time spent at work seen as acceptable?	Is corporate communication regarded as good?	Does the way they are described support this?	How do salaries compare with competitive organizations?
What rules govern their behaviour? (Everything from dress and smoking policy to use of company equipment)*	Does the manager consult?	Do people collaborate?	Are there additional facilities that are regarded as necessary?	Are social facilities provided for staff (and appreciated by them)?	Are objectives used appropriately?	What recognition is there of long service or special expertise?	Are prevailing levels reviewed regularly?
	How is the manager rated?	Is collaboration expected, appreciated and does it help?	Do people regard suggestions for change as being well considered?	Does management make allowances for special effort that affects home life?	Is management seen as suitably strong?	Do staff feel management supports their position within the organization as a whole?	Are appraisals a basis for this consideration and how are they regarded?

*NOTE such questions may need answering twice: once with regard to company-wide policy, and again with regard to the departmental or more sectional situations which may well be different in nature.

a foundation for action

If something that will be seen as negative is going to happen (even for the best of reasons) then action must be ready for the event. Say a part of the organization is to be closed or scaled down. This will certainly seem negative: people may see others losing their job or adversely affected even if they stay, they may imagine worse is to come, that this is the start of something and that the next stage will affect them directly. Incidentally, the reaction will always stem from a combination of genuine facts and other things feared or imagined, or both. Given that management knows what is coming, communication (real information and explanation) and compensating action must start ahead of the closure and aim to balance the effect. A dip in motivation may be inevitable. But it can perhaps be short-lived, and made a dip rather than a veritable mineshaft. To continue the example, perhaps a closure is part of a longer-term plan to concentrate and grow other aspects of the business – in which case after a dip motivation may actually rise once the truth of the intention is seen. Even if it is the lesser of two evils, perhaps, then management action can keep views of it in perspective and prevent any major impact on performance as a result.

Equally such events may be positive. Maybe the company is opening new branches and everyone will benefit from the growth. Here then the job is to use a positive situation to boost motivation. There is a difference between just allowing good news to flow out naturally and feeling that it will, by definition, produce good feelings and that there is nothing else to do. The effect can be made specific. So it is good news – but what *exactly* will it mean for people? Spelling it out may well enhance a general good feeling and make it more powerful.

Sometimes too the event will be external. For example, a publisher might participate in the London Book Fair, a major event in the industry. Everyone might know the date – but again the detail matters: why should those who attend find it interesting or valuable? And how can those who stay in the office, coping with more than usual because half the people in the company are out, be made to feel good about their role? Anticipation can help whatever the circumstances. So, motivation needs planning as well as ideas. Any lack here can cause real problems.

the dangers

Apart from the danger, mentioned above, of missing, through lack of anticipation, major events and being unable to compensate for them (if they are negative), the main danger is of falling into a very ad hoc style of motivation. It is all too easy to recognize at some point that someone, or some group, has been neglected. It may well be for what are superficially very good reasons. All has been going well, no meetings or even much communication has been necessary – and perhaps this has been exaggerated by absences: holidays, business trips, training courses, etc taken by either party. From the perspective of the person neglected it may well be that this is seen in very clear cut terms, for example as a sign of:

- ■ lack of interest;
- ■ dislike;
- ■ the unimportance of their role;
- ■ unfavourable comparisons: other people or tasks being seen as more important;
- ■ a focus on the negative ('I only ever see the boss when something is wrong').

The last is especially important. People quickly develop negative feelings about what should be positive things if the only communications they are involved in are problem-orientated.

The moral is clear: motivation needs to be approached systematically in order to maximize its effectiveness. How is this achieved? Several avenues are open to you that promote this.

positive habits

Habits are powerful. Think of something you do that has really become a firm habit. It might be something simple like checking you have a key in a particular pocket before leaving your house or office. It might be more complex like your approach to a repeating task: for example the way I prepare for a presentation or training assignment follows something of a pattern (one designed to make preparation effective, but minimize the time it takes). You can no doubt think of things like this that apply to yourself. The point is that such things can save time and increase effectiveness, yet remove the need to constantly reinvent the wheel.

Certainly simple things like saying 'Well done', or its equivalent, can be viewed in a way that acts to cultivate their becoming a habit. The intention is not that something is then done unthinkingly. The habit does not prevent an action being applied with some consideration, indeed it should be – it is not going to ring true if your habit means your 'Well dones' come across with a mechanistic feel, on a par with the worst delivered examples of 'Have a nice day'. But a habit can act to prompt the deployment of specific actions, enabling a little consideration to then ensure that exactly how it is deployed makes its mark.

a motivational calendar

A simple planning chart can assist in smoothing the motivational inputs you should make in a simple way. An annual planner, either something linked to a diary and the calendar year or a more flexible system (like Filofax) that means you keep whatever number of months ahead you find useful, is all that is necessary. These days, of course, there might well be what you regard as a more convenient alternative on a computer or personal organizer. Notes made on such a system fall into two categories, shown here with a few examples.

events

Here you list events that will affect people and influence their motivational feelings. The following are examples, listed with reasons why they could be important:

- *calendar events:* Christmas, Easter, summer holidays (preceded by a hectic period when special motivation is useful);
- *personal events:* birthdays, anniversaries – including such as 10 years with the organization, taking an exam or gaining a qualification (congratulations – or more – may be in order and the fact that such are remembered may itself be useful);
- *corporate events:* changes to the organization, new recruits joining, or others leaving, the start of new procedures, initiatives or more major events such as a merger or takeover (where such must be preceded or accompanied by motivational action);
- *communications events:* publication of a company staff magazine to tie in with a particular meeting (with an opportunity to tie in for motivational purposes).

actions

Here you list actions that will be part of your personal work, thus:

■ *systems change:* changing a form or reporting system, adding, rescinding or changing rules or standing instructions (thus if a change is likely to be difficult to understand or felt to be a bad thing, motivational action can be planned and taken to compensate);

■ *communications:* something like the planned circulation of an annual plan or the scheduling of an annual staff conference (which might well need motivational action in parallel);

■ *personal focus:* if you are going to be away, or spending time on some crash programme to the exclusion of other considerations this may affect others around you – who may, for instance, have take over other parts of your workload (here people may need to be persuaded to co-operate and the change needs to be made to seem attractive).

Such examples are not, of course, mutually exclusive. A simple, specific example fills in some detail. Imagine that one of your team is being promoted. This in itself is likely to be motivational; however, when you take the action may help maximize the effect, and your chart may prompt a good decision about scheduling the announcement. This might be at a time when: the announcement can go promptly in a company newsletter or be more broadly notified (eg to customers, with a mailing imminent), they can join a management committee they will now be a member of without delay. Or the timing might be influenced by others in the organization – when will the announcement best impact on their peers, for example. Or by personal matters: the timing might allow a promotion to be announced on someone's birthday. Such principles can be applied whatever the circumstances; the more important the event or action the more you may gain from this sort of analysis.

Also on the calendar, but worth a specific word, are *communications opportunities.* The continuity of individual and group contact is important. When, how often and with what frequency do meetings take place? Is this increased by social or semi-social contacts? In what corporate events do people participate? Again the continuity is important and this style of planning will help avoid unwarranted gaps, build communications one upon another and ensure that communication, which is a fundamental element of all motivation, works well. Whatever is on your calendar, and only a few notes are necessary; being able to see them 'in the round' and easily relate one thing to another is also useful.

individual records

In addition to a calendar, at the other end of the scale in fact, another worthwhile record is one that charts your situation with each individual member of your team. Some motivational action, as we have reviewed, can be directed at a group of people; much, however, is by definition individual. Here all that is necessary is a page (diary sheet, computer screen – whatever) per person.

Many managers keep such a record with regard to development, charting training and development needs, projects in progress and plans for the future, both short and longer term. If this is done – and it is to be highly recommended – then some notes about motivation sit very neatly alongside it. It is especially important that the terms used act as a memory jogger that allows you to fulfil promises made. For example, if you say to someone that you must have a word when they come back from attending a course, then, provided your style of management is constructive, people will look forward to it. It is an opportunity to link the training experience to the job and particularly to how things are handled in future; after all, good training should prompt ideas and prompt new ways of approaching and doing things.

If such a session does not materialize, and materialize promptly, then a person will feel let down. They are likely to read negative motives into it – 'They can't be bothered', 'I'm not important enough for them to take time over this' – and instead of an opportunity for motivation being effective, not only does nothing positive happen but, at worst, a step backwards is taken.

A note of your intentions for an individual, recorded and consulted regularly, can thus be invaluable. No great effort or time is necessary to keep it up, and it is precisely the kind of thing that becomes a routine – and the more useful you find it the easier it is to resolve to keep it up.

spontaneity

Having touched on systems and routines it is important not to give the impression that everything should be done to a formula, as it were. If your every motivational effort seems to come off a checklist then its impact will be diluted. At worst people will see it as cynical and worth nothing. There is a trite American expression which says in so many words: 'Be sincere, whether you mean it or not'. Awful. And certainly untrue; people can spot insincerity at 100 paces. They have to feel you care, and indeed you *must* care if you are to motivate success-fully. If you have a good team, then this should not be a problem; you will *want* to look after them.

What is necessary is having a spontaneous element in your motivational action (and in other aspects of your management style too perhaps). It is one thing to plan, let us say, a depart-mental dinner linked to the annual sales conference. It can be motivational and the fact that it has clearly been timed to fit with such an event is seen as logical and does not dilute the impact.

But once in a while it is worth gathering people together unexpectedly and saying something like: 'We have had a great month, you've all worked very hard, so let's…' and suggesting a treat. The effect may not be greater than the planned occasion, but it is different in nature, and ringing the changes to enhance motivation has been mentioned before. Similarly with a host of things, including a brief, unexpected, note.

a rolling plan

In these kinds of ways you can plan to motivate and make sure that what you plan and how you fit it in creates the effect you want. It should be what is often called a 'rolling' plan, meaning that it is not set in tablets of stone. The plan, the notes and prompts that you record point the direction you want to go.

As you look ahead what the plan says changes in nature. For instance, thus:

■ *For the next three months:* it sets out perhaps 60–70 per cent of what you will do. Details need to be filled in and some of what will happen must be added, so too must thoughts about exactly how things will be done.

■ *For the following three months:* the proportion of what is decided and its timing will be less and more detail needs to be added and fine-tuned; but there is time to do just that.

■ *For the rest of a twelve-month period:* it sets out just an outline of what you will do; major events and their timing are set and may not change, but the rest of what must be done awaits further thought, changing circumstances and events.

Such approaches avoid the ad hoc dangers suggested at the start of this chapter and, as with so much else in management, show the value of preparation rather than making it all up as you go. The concept of a plan lays the responsibility for motivating people firmly where it belongs – with the line managers to whom they report. More senior levels can play their part too, and the principles for their involvement are similar.

But with regard to your people the job is yours. The time you need to spend on motivation stacks up well against the potential rewards. Effective motivation makes a difference. And it is a pity to have things firing on less than the full number of cylinders, as it were. Remember that there are always more chrysalises than there are butterflies – you just have to make sure they are encouraged to hatch; and to fly.

afterword

If you think you can, you can and if you think you can't, you're right.

Mary Kay Ash

At this point it is worth taking stock. In dissecting any process, certainly one with as many aspects to it as motivating people, there is a danger that the complexities pile up, leaving one with a feeling that it is all somewhat difficult. Yet some things are entirely straightforward. All managers are ultimately judged on their results. Whether you manage one other person, a small team or an entire organization, you are dependent on the contribution others make as much, if not more, than on what you do yourself. And the quality of others' contribution is dependent on their motivation. People perform better when their motivation is high. What is more the difference between adequate performance and excellent performance spurred on by motivation can be considerable.

So motivation works, but – despite this – it is sometimes neglected. If so, this is less likely to be because a manager has tried and failed, more because he or she has found the process difficult or inconvenient and given up on it. It is an area where half measures are likely not just to fail to achieve what you want, but be seen as inadequate by those towards whom they are directed; they can end up being part of what is regarded as an overall negative influence.

In fact, as this short book has been at pains to demonstrate, motivation need not be difficult. The principles are common sense and there are plenty of ideas for action – many of them individually simple and straightforward – to help create a powerful, continuous positive motivational effect.

Like most managers, you are no doubt busy. The greatest difficulty about motivation is perhaps simply the perceived difficulty of fitting it in. Yet the rewards make the time it takes well worthwhile, and the effect of the problems of a demotivated group of people on their manager's time are all too obvious.

Successful managers are good at motivation. What is most important then? Without meaning to negate other thoughts expressed throughout the book, 10 keys to successfully adopting a motivational management style may be summarized as follows:

1. Always think about the people aspects of everything.
2. Keep a list of possible motivational actions, large and small, in mind.
3. Monitor the 'motivational temperature' regularly.
4. See the process as continuous and cumulative.
5. Ring the changes in terms of method to maintain interest.
6. Do not be censorious about what motivates others, either positively or negatively.
7. Beware of panaceas and easy options.
8. Make sufficient time for it.
9. Evaluate what works best within your group.
10. Remember that, in part at least, there should be a 'fun' aspect to work (and that it is your job to make sure this is so).

If you make motivation a habit, and go about it in the right way, you may be surprised by what you can achieve with it. The motivation for you to motivate others is in the results. If

10 things seem too many to keep in mind, let us end by concentrating on three, perhaps more overall, factors. Motivational action must be:

■ *Well judged* Improving motivation is not simply about ensuring employees have everything they want. Maybe everyone would like a large office, two secretaries and unlimited expenses, but that is not the way organizational life is. Action must recognize a host of practical issues, and also take into account what the cost of any changes may be.

■ *Creative* Ideas for action need thought, may be better for debate among a number of people, and are rarely as simple as just reiterating the old formula. Taking the time and trouble to seek out new solutions is often very worthwhile.

■ *Balanced* As was made clear in the Introduction, motivation is the very opposite of the application of magic solutions – still less one specific magic formula. What works best is always going to be a mixture of different things, a fact that any more detailed investigation of the theory and practice involved will bear out. Assembling this mix (and not being censorious about any aspect of it) is the way to success.

Beyond the above there is perhaps one word that characterizes the motivational process better than any other. That is the fact that the process is *continuous*. The observation and measurement of the prevailing motivational climate must be regular; action to maintain or improve it must be too. Given that, the results that it all influences will flow through on a regular basis too. And, at the end of the day, management is about producing results – through other people.

So, if you have read this far – well done. If you are now resolved to be more active in your motivational action – well done again. If you have a list of actions you want to take or areas you are resolved to consider further (which is the best possible way to end any review) – another well done, though such thoughts need progressing and linking to ongoing action. Try even one new thing and its working may well encourage you to try more. The first step is the most difficult. If later, having made some changes, you find the motivation of the people you work with improving, and their results following the same path, that is down to you – and you can congratulate both your people and yourself for making it happen.